The Palestinian State

In recent years interest in the Middle East crisis has been increasing. The conflict between Israelis and Palestinians is a constant theme in the media. The images of heavily armed soldiers facing young Palestinian children hurling stones have evoked dismay and alarm. In this concise book, Dan Cohn-Sherbok, an American-born Reform rabbi and Professor of Judaism, argues for a two-state solution to this seemingly intractable problem. Drawing on the Jewish ethical tradition, he maintains that Jews world-wide must now press for the creation of a Palestinian state in the Holy Land. In the shadow of the Holocaust, the empowered must empower those who seek nationhood, before it is too late.

Dan Cohn-Sherbok is Professor Emeritus of Judaism at the University of Wales; Honorary Professor at Aberystwyth University; Visiting Professor at York St John University and St Mary's University College; and Visiting Research Fellow at Heythrop College, University of London. He is the author of numerous books dealing with contemporary Judaism including *Israel: The History of an Idea; The Palestinian–Israeli Conflict* (with Dawoud El-Alami); and *Introduction to Zionism and Israel: From Ideology to History*.

'This book is an interesting and timely analysis of the Arab-Israeli conflict. From the Jewish perspective, it is based in part on moderate and mainstream Jewish religious principles, and reaches sensible and realistic conclusions centred around the necessity for a two-state solution to this seemingly intractible dispute. It can be highly recommended as an intelligent and balanced overview.'

William D. Rubinstein, Emeritus Professor of History, University of Aberystwyth

'Containing a fair-minded, short history of the conflict between the Arabs and Israelis, the main strength of this book lies in its authorship by a Jew, and not just any Jew: a rabbi and theologian who is immersed in the best traditions of Judaic humanism. Although he belongs to the liberal Reform wing of Judaism, Professor Cohn-Sherbok's loyalty to the state of Israel cannot be doubted by the Orthodox or the hardline, precisely those who hold the key to the future of peace in the region. He draws on the teachings of their faith to inspire them to make as many concessions as are compatible with security to lessen the appeal of Arab and Islamic extremists among the Palestinians to help to bring about a two-state solution to this long-festering wound.'

Hazhir Teimourian, broadcaster and writer, Middle Eastern politics and history

'In this thoughtful and engaging work, Dan Cohn-Sherbok provides a compelling argument for an Israel and Palestine that live side by side in peace and security. Arguing from the Jewish tradition of ethics and compassion, while remaining mindful of the tumultuous Jewish past, Cohn-Sherbok views a Palestinian state as necessary for Palestinians *and* Jews. At a time when the two-state solution seems to be slipping away, Cohn-Sherbok's profoundly human moderation should be listened to and heeded.'

Marc H. Ellis, University Professor of Jewish Studies, Professor of History, Director of the Center for Jewish Studies at Baylor University

'*The Palestinian State* by Rabbi Dan Cohn-Sherbok provides a vital and timely contribution toward the search for justice and peace in the Middle East, from a religious Jewish perspective. Written by a Jewish rabbi, the title is intentionally provocative but sums up his hopes for peace with justice for Jews and Palestinians. Security for Israel is linked to justice for Palestinians.

When the Zionist colonisation of Palestine is increasingly being driven by Orthodox settlers who claim divine authority for their exclusive and expansionist agenda, Dan Cohn-Sherbok draws attention to an alternative and beautiful Jewish liberation theology, rooted firmly in the Hebrew scriptures.

Dan Cohn-Sherbok shows that at the heart of the Hebrew canon is an ethical tradition that respects human dignity, and recognises the intrinsic equality of Jews and Palestinians since both are created in the image and likeness of God. The Passover not only looks back to the liberation of the Hebrews from slavery, but points forward and should inspire compassion for Palestinians who long to escape from exile too. Similarly, the imperative of the Hebrew prophets demands equality for all, which today requires justice and mercy toward Palestinian aspirations for self determination and a home-land of their own.

Time is running out to resolve the Arab–Israeli conflict, in part because people tend to hold polarised and entrenched positions. It is therefore difficult to hear the cry or feel the pain felt by the other side. Empathy is in short supply. Pessimism is common currency. Distrust in diplomacy is growing. Interminable peace negotiations are leading to cynicism. Hopelessness and despair, especially among the young, is breeding radicalism and fermenting violent extremism on both sides.

For those holding entrenched positions, this book may well make for uncomfortable reading because Dan Cohn-Sherbok presents the history and aspirations of both sides with fairness and compassion. It is therefore essential reading for those who believe the 'unsolv-able' can be solved.

I share Dan Cohn-Sherbok's view that an inclusive and lasting peace in the Middle East is truly possible because it reflects the heart and will of God.'

Revd Dr Stephen Sizer, author of *Christian Zionism:*
Road-Map to Armageddon?

'With great courage and an overwhelming sense of moral urgency Professor Dan Cohn Sherbok sets out a compelling case for the need for a Palestinian State. What makes this a book such an original contribution is Rabbi Cohn Sherbok's rootedness in the strong ethical traditions of Judaism. There are many accounts elsewhere of the origins of the Palestinian/Israeli conflict – usually with a heavy bias to one side or another. Yet this book sets out its case – in a calm, compassionate manner – not only that the only solution is that the Palestinians be granted a state, but that this follows from the most profound principles of Judaism: its belief in the Kingdom of God. It is not politics that offers a solution, but a moral praxis at the heart of faith. In a situation where many have already given up hope for a peaceful end to conflict, this book demonstrates that there are still new avenues to explore, still arguments that "guide our feet in the ways of peace".'

Professor Mary Grey, Visiting Professor, St Mary's University College; Honorary Professor, University of Winchester

'This basic primer will not please those who dislike complexity and prefer a black and white rendition of history . . . it is indeed complex and not simple. Not so much Israel against Palestine or vice-versa, but the rationalists in both camps against their rejectionists.'

Colin Shindler, Emeritus Professor, SOAS, University of London, Chairman of the European Association of Israel Studies

The Palestinian State

A Jewish Justification

Dan Cohn-Sherbok

IMPRESS
BOOKS

First Published 2012
by Impress Books Ltd

Innovation Centre, Rennes Drive, University of Exeter Campus,
Exeter EX4 4RN

© Dan Cohn-Sherbok 2012

Typeset in Sabon by Swales & Willis Ltd, Exeter, Devon

Printed and bound in England by imprintdigital.net

British Library Cataloguing in Publication Data
A catalogue record for this book is available from the British Library

ISBN 13: 978–1–907–60529–1 (paperback)
ISBN 13: 978–1–907–60530–7 (ebook)

For Lavinia

For decades, there has been a stalemate: two peoples with legitimate aspirations, each with a painful history that makes compromise elusive. It is easy to point fingers – for Palestinians to point to the displacement brought by Israel's founding, and for Israelis to point to the constant hostility and attacks throughout its history from within its borders as well as beyond. But if we see this conflict only from one side or the other, then we will be blind to the truth: the only resolution is for the aspirations of both sides to be met through two states, where Israelis and Palestinians each live in peace and security.

President Barack Obama
(Speech delivered in Cairo on 4 June, 2009)

Contents

Preface

I have had the pleasure and the privilege of working with Dan Cohn-Sherbok over a number of years. We have exchanged ideas and information, and I like to believe that we have learned a great deal from each other during this time. For several years Dan and I ran parallel undergraduate courses at the University of Wales, Lampeter on the State of Israel and the Palestinian Question respectively. We held regular talks and debates both within the university and for external interest groups and we wrote a book together designed to give a simple historical introduction to the subject for non-specialists and to present the key arguments for both sides. The reception that this book received in its first and subsequent updated editions has convinced us that there is genuine interest in this subject and that there are many people both within and outside the two communities who wish both peoples well and who would like to see a just and peaceful solution to what appears to be an intractable problem.

Dan and I come to this subject from different political and cultural perspectives but both of us recognize that dialogue is essential. It does not strengthen our own claims for protection of our human and political rights to deny those of others, and it does not validate our own historical perspectives to attack or undermine the documented or received narrative history of the other.

Dan has a gift for extracting key themes from complex topics and presenting them in an informative and accessible form to the general reader. This work opens with a clear exposition of the ethical foundations of Jewish theology and God's commandment to Jews to create the Kingdom of God founded on justice and righteousness. Quoting from Scripture and rabbinical literature he emphasizes the importance of truth, justice, charity, human freedom and dignity, protection of the weak and the equality and solidarity of human beings. He goes on to analyse in the second chapter the biblical event that is perhaps the most significant and symbolic to the Jewish people, the deliverance from Egypt. He discusses the importance of the remembrance of this, its meaning as the core of a Jewish liberation theology and the universality of its application. Freedom from tyranny and oppression are at the centre of the Jewish consciousness and this should lead Jews to stand up for freedom and dignity for all people. Theory alone is not enough, however, and he goes on to make the point that it has always been understood that the principles on which the faith is founded must be enacted in daily life, in every day morality and in practical, ethical politics. This means acknowledging the suffering of others and reaching out to the oppressed and the dispossessed.

This is a leap of faith. Dan has a deep commitment to the concept of the State of Israel. As the shadow of the Holocaust still looms large over the lives of so many people, he sees the existence of the Jewish homeland as a guarantee and safeguard for the Jewish people against the possibility of any future genocide. So long as there is a place of refuge where Jews are the majority, they will never be forced to suffer as a powerless minority in another country. No one would wish to deny the Jewish people this protection. Dan recognizes, however, that what a community wishes for itself it should also wish for others. Drawing on the prophetic tradition and the Jewish people's experience of diaspora and disempowerment, he makes the argument that the Palestinian people are equally entitled to a homeland and to security and self-determination.

This is not only a moral position but a practical necessity. There can be no hope for peace while the Palestinians remain deprived of any recognized political identity or representation in the international arena. Dan argues that Jews world-wide should support the proposition of a two-state solution and UN recognition of Palestinian statehood in principle. He suggests that this need not specify borders in the first instance as its importance would be as an expression of good faith and commitment to a long-term, peaceful solution. At the same time, for Israel to have confidence to move forward, there would have to be a commitment to peace on the part of the Palestinians in order to ensure the security of Israel and to reassure Israelis and Israel's external supporters that there will be no holocaust in the Holy Land. Both communities have deeply rooted historical, religious and cultural connections to the Holy Land and progress will only be possible when each acknowledges the validity of these connections and the equal humanity of the other. Both communities have suffered, and it is natural for this to create the determination to survive and to ensure that this will never happen to us again. But suffering should also bring us to understanding and compassion and the desire to relieve the suffering of others. It is this tradition of compassion in Judaism that Dan draws on in the search for a prospect for peace.

In the process of working together, Dan and I have become firm friends. We have agreed to disagree on certain points and we could debate interpretations of historical events endlessly, but this would not move us a single step forward. I believe, however, that we do agree on the bigger picture - that the conflict does not have to destroy the lives of any more generations of Israeli or Palestinian children. The security and prosperity of each is dependent upon the other. There are divisions within both communities, and each is burdened with the agendas and expectations of others, but in both communities there are those who are driven to seek a better future for all. We can but hope that people on both sides may find encouragement in this humane and courageous work.

Dawoud El-Alami

4 January 2012

Dawoud El-Alami is from an old Palestinian family but was brought up in Egypt and has lived and worked in the UK for twenty-five years. He has taught at the universities of Kent and Oxford and the University of Wales, Lampeter and although his main academic interest is in Islamic family law, he has an active interest in the Israel–Palestine question.

Acknowledgements

I would like to acknowledge my indebtedness to: Dawoud El-Alami (with Dan Cohn-Sherbok) *The Palestine–Israeli Conflict*, Oxford, Oneworld, 2006); Benny Morris, *One State, Two States: Resolving the Israel/Palestine Conlict*, London, Yale University Press, 2009; Avi Shlaim, *Israel and Palestine*, London, Verso, 2010; Marc Ellis, *Towards a Jewish Theology of Liberation*, Baylor, Baylor University Press, 2004; Martin Gilbert, *Israel: A History*, London, Black Swan, 1999; Conor Cruise O'Brien, *The Seige: The Saga of Israel and Zionism*, London, Paladin, 1988; Howard M. Sachar, *A History of Israel from the Rise of Zionism to Our Time*, New York, Alfred A. Knof, 2007. I would also like to thank Routledge for permission to use maps from Dan Cohn-Sherbok, *Judaism: History, Belief and Practice*, London, Routledge, 2003.

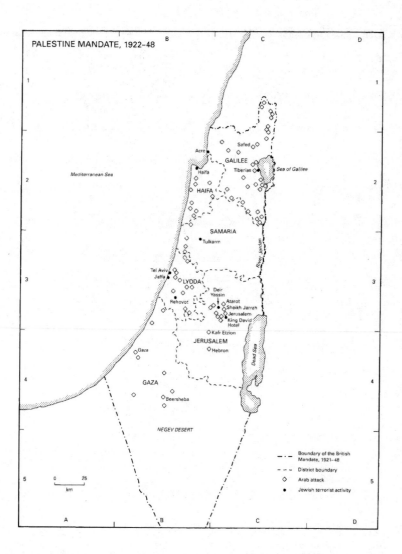

PALESTINE MANDATE, 1922–48

Mediterranean Sea

Acre
Safed
GALILEE
Haifa
Tiberias
Sea of Galilee
HAIFA

SAMARIA
Tulkarm
River Jordan

Tel Aviv
Jaffa
LYDDA
Deir
Yassin
Atarot
Rehovot
Sheikh Jarrah
Jerusalem
King David
Hotel
Kafr Etzion
JERUSALEM
Hebron
Dead Sea

Gaza

GAZA
Beersheba

NEGEV DESERT

Boundary of the British
Mandate, 1921–48
District boundary
Arab attack
Jewish terrorist activity

0   25
km

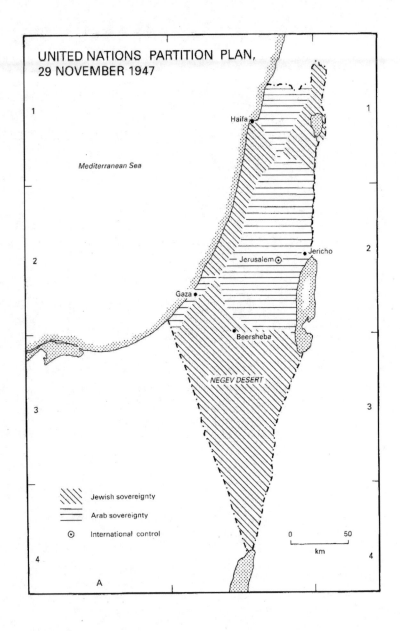

UNITED NATIONS PARTITION PLAN,
29 NOVEMBER 1947

Mediterranean Sea

Haifa

Jericho
Jerusalem ⊙

Gaza

Beersheba

NEGEV DESERT

Jewish sovereignty

Arab sovereignty

⊙ International control

0   50
km

A

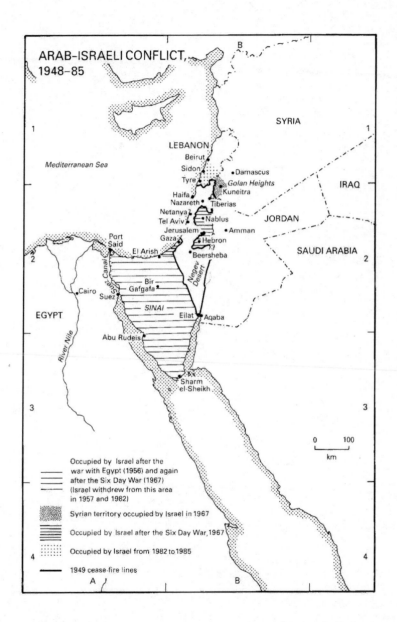

ARAB-ISRAELI CONFLICT,
1948-85

SYRIA

1

Mediterranean Sea

LEBANON

Beirut

Sidon
•Damascus

Tyre
Golan Heights

Haifa
Kuneitra

Nazareth
Tiberias

Netanya
Nablus

Tel Aviv

Jerusalem
•Amman

Gaza
Hebron

El Arish
Beersheba

Port
Said

2

Negev Desert

Bir
Gafgafa

•Cairo
SINAI

Suez

Eilat
Aqaba

EGYPT

Abu Rudeis

River Nile

Sharm
el-Sheikh

3

IRAQ

JORDAN

SAUDI ARABIA

0   100

km

Occupied by Israel after the
war with Egypt (1956) and again
after the Six Day War (1967)
(Israel withdrew from this area
in 1957 and 1982)

Syrian territory occupied by Israel in 1967

Occupied by Israel after the Six Day War, 1967

Occupied by Israel from 1982 to 1985

1949 cease-fire lines

4

A   B

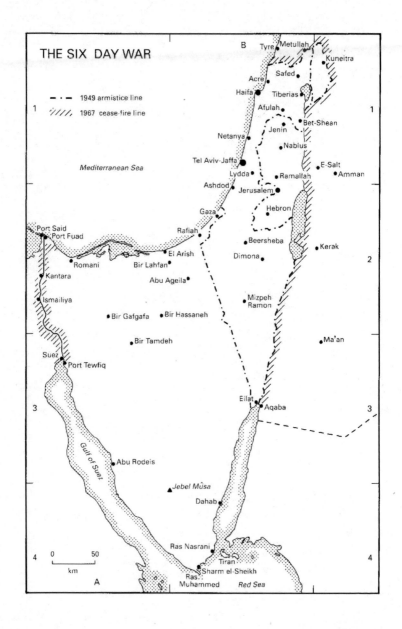

THE SIX DAY WAR

- · - · -   1949 armistice line
/////   1967 cease-fire line

Mediterranean Sea

Port Said
Port Fuad
Romani
Kantara
Ismailiya
Suez
Port Tewfiq

Gulf of Suez

El Arish
Bir Lahfan
Abu Ageila
Bir Gafgafa
Bir Hassaneh
Bir Tamdeh

Abu Rodeis

▲ *Jebel Mûsa*

Dahab

Ras Nasrani
Tiran
Sharm el-Sheikh
Ras Muhammed
Red Sea

B
Tyre
Metullah
Kuneitra
Acre
Safed
Haifa
Tiberias
Afulah
Bet-Shean
Netanya
Jenin
Nablus
Tel Aviv-Jaffa
E-Salt
Lydda
Ramallah
Amman
Ashdod
Jerusalem
Gaza
Hebron
Rafiah
Beersheba
Kerak
Dimona
Mizpeh Ramon
Ma'an

Eilat
Aqaba

0   50
km

A

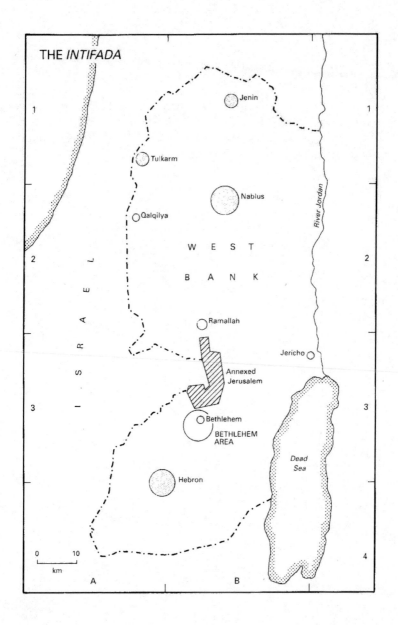

THE *INTIFADA*

Jenin

Tulkarm

Nablus

Qalqilya

W E S T

B A N K

Ramallah

Jericho

Annexed
Jerusalem

Bethlehem

BETHLEHEM
AREA

Hebron

Dead
Sea

I S R A E L

River Jordan

0   10

km

1

2

3

4

A   B

The Palestinian State Website Companion

A website companion to this volume can be found at www.impress-books.co.uk/Palestine. The companion is an A–Z directory of informative websites dealing with the Israeli-Palestine conflict compiled and updated by the author.

Introduction:
From Holocaust to Liberation

A little before seven, there was an announcement: 'The first train will arrive in ten minute!' A few minutes later a train arrived from Lemberg: forty-five carriages with more than six thousand people . . . A loudspeaker gave instructions: 'Strip, even artificial limbs and glasses. Hand all money and valuables in at the "valuables" window'. . . Stark naked men, women and children and cripples passed by . . . SS men pushed the men into chambers . . . Seven to eight hundred people in ninety-three square meters. The doors closed . . . Twenty-five minutes passed. You could see through the windows that many were already dead, for an electric light illuminated the interior of the room . . . All were dead after thirty-two minutes . . . The people were still standing like columns of stone, with no room to fall or lean. Even in death you could tell the families, all holding hands. . . .

(Nuremberg document PS-2170)

Only seventy years ago millions of Jews lost their lives in such a fashion. Yet the people survived the Nazi onslaught. And once Hitler had been defeated, the Jewish community affirmed its

1

commitment to Jewish survival through the establishment of a homeland in Palestine. Having emerged from the prospect of annihilation, the Jewish nation has flourished in Israel and elsewhere.

Nonetheless, the nightmare of the Holocaust continues to haunt Jewry-it has deepened the Jewish determination to defend Israel and ensure that Jews everywhere are protected from antisemitic attack. Further, the murder of millions of Jews at the hands of the Nazis has persuaded many Jews that Jewish self-interest must prevail over all other concerns. For most Jews today, what is required is a commitment to the continuation of Judaism and the Jewish nation.

Such an attitude has been most eloquently expressed by the Jewish theologian Emil Fackenheim, who insisted that it is a sacred duty to respond to the Holocaust. The intention of the Nazis was to eliminate all Jews. No survivor was to be left to tell the story of what horrors that took place. However, Fackenheim insisted that in the death camps the Voice of God was heard. Out of the ashes of the crematoria God issued a further command. This 614th commandment is directed to the post-Holocaust Jewish community. According to Fackenheim:

> Jews are forbidden to hand Hitler posthumous victories. They are commanded to survive as Jews, lest the Jewish people perish. They are commanded to remember the victims of Auschwitz lest their memory perish. They are forbidden to despair of man and his world, and to escape into either cynicism or other worldliness, lest they co-operate in delivering the world over to the forces of Auschwitz. Finally, they are forbidden to despair of the God of Israel, lest Judaism perish ... A Jew may not respond to Hitler's attempt to destroy Judaism by himself co-operating in its destruction. In ancient times, the unthinkable Jewish sin was idolatry. Today it is to respond by doing his work.
>
> (Emil Fackenheim, 'Jewish Faith and the Holocaust',
> in Michael Morgan (ed.), *The Jewish Thought
> of Emil Fackenheim*, p. 176)

In this theological formulation, Fackenheim has given voice to a universal sentiment expressed by contemporary Jewry: Never Again!

In a post-Holocaust world, the quest for Jewish survival has under-standably eclipsed all other matters. However, such a focus of Jew-ish life has turned Jewry inwards – in its determination to endure at all costs, the universal truths of biblical and rabbinic Judaism have been suppressed. The Jewish preoccupation with survival has tended to blind the Jewish people to the needs of those non-Jews who are presently undergoing hardship similar to that which the Jewish people endured through the centuries. In this respect, con-temporary Jewry has lost sight of the prophetic vision of the Jewish people as a light to the nations. In particular, in the struggle to over-come the tragedy of the Holocaust, the Jewish nation has turned its face against the sufferings of the Palestinian people. What is now needed is for the empowered to empower the homeless: it is time for the Palestinians to have a state of their own.

Most discussions of the Middle East crisis focus on the politi-cal and social dimensions of the Israeli–Palestinian crisis. Yet, as Jews, it is imperative that we view the conflict between Israelis and Palestinians in a religious context. In this regard, the starting point of Jewish theological reflection is the plight of those who remain in exile. A Jewish theology of liberation claims that God is to be found in the situation of those who are currently suffering depriva-tion and depersonalization, just as in Scripture God is the redeemer and saviour of those who are enslaved. What is required is solidar-ity with those who suffer. The problems of those at the margin of society should become our own. The vocation of every Jew is to opt for human love and compassion.

Part I, thus, is concerned with the theological and moral dimen-sions of the Jewish tradition as a background to the conflict in the Middle East. Chapter 1 focuses on the Jewish concept of the King-dom of God as found in both the Bible and the rabbinic tradition. In Scripture, God is portrayed as the king who rights injustice. He is the enthroned sovereign who protects the weak and rescues those who suffer, acting justly and with mercy. Developing this tradi-tion, rabbinic sages envisaged God as the supreme ruler who calls all people to bring about the divine Kingdom on earth. Accord-ing to tradition, this will take place in this world, and each person has responsibility for undertaking such a transformation of society. Obedience to God's commandments is paramount. For the rabbis, the Kingdom of God consists in a complete moral order built on the principles of trust, righteousness and holiness among all nations. Humanity is thus at the centre of creation. Only God's creatures can make the Kingdom glorious: this is a divinely appointed task in which the Jewish people play a central role.

Chapter 2 continues this discussion, stressing the significance of the Exodus narrative. According to the Book of Exodus, in ancient times God rescued the Jewish people from slavery in Egypt. In the biblical account, God is on the side of the oppressed; remembering the covenant with his chosen people, he delivered the ancient Hebrews from bondage. For Jews the profundity of the Exodus account consists in its significance for the present. Every year at Passover, Jews are reminded of their responsibility for others. Any Jew who sits down to the Passover meal and is oblivious to the plight of those who are oppressed has missed the meaning of the celebration. The keynote of the Haggadah is that persecution and divine deliverance are contemporary realities. In rabbinic literature, the sages stress that the God of Israel is the God of the living not of the dead. He is attentive to those who seek deliverance, just as he listened to the cry of the Jewish people in Egypt. The Passover meal is thus a symbol of Israel's vocation; as Jews recall their suffering and deliverance, they must heed the cry of those suffer in the modern world.

As Chapter 3 explains, the Jewish faith is rooted in practical action. History is of critical importance. From ancient times, Jews have expressed their longing for the coming of God's Kingdom in which truth, justice and righteousness will prevail. This is the goal of history. God as a moral being demands moral living. In the classic religious texts of Judaism, moral behaviour is a predominant theme. The Jewish religion does not insist on the acceptance of formal theological dogma; orthopraxis – rather than theological orthodoxy – is critical. In the history of the nation, there has never been a central body that has laid down a religious creed. Rather the books of the Bible and early rabbinic literature contain beliefs about God's nature and activity, yet neither the Bible, the Mishnah nor the collections of midrashim contain an elaborately formulated series of beliefs. Instead, religious texts present God as active in the world. In later rabbinic sources, Jewish thinkers continued to debate about the central principles of Judaism, yet there was universal agreement about the significance of moral action. For the Jew, observance rather than belief is regarded as authoritative. True faith consists not in an affirmation of belief, but in commitment to repairing the world (*tikkun olam*) in accordance with God's demands.

In the light of such ethical demands, Part II focuses on the Middle East conflict as it has evolved over the last hundred years. Chapter 4 – written from a Jewish perspective – begins with a brief account of the Zionist quest for a homeland for Jewry. Through the efforts of Theodor Herzl, attempts were made to persuade the British to authorize Jewish settlement in Palestine. Eventually in 1917, the British government issued the Balfour Declaration which favoured the establishment of a national home for the Jewish people. Yet, with the rise of Arab nationalism, the Jewish community was continually under attack. In 1947 the United Nations voted to partition Palestine and the following year the Israeli Declaration of Independence was read out by David Ben-Gurion in the Tel Aviv Museum. Immediately, Israel was attacked. This war was followed by a series of violent conflicts between Israel and the Arab world. Numerous attempts have been made to resolve this seemingly insoluble problem, but no solution has been achieved.

Today the Palestinian people long for statehood, and Chapter 5 presents the Palestinian argument. Initially the Ottoman Empire welcomed Jews to Palestine, and by the middle of the nineteenth century the Jewish community numbered about 10,000. However, once Arabs became aware of the Zionist intention to create a sizable homeland in Palestine, the indigenous population became increasingly alarmed. In their view, Britain had no right to issue the Balfour Declaration of 1917 – no foreign government, they argued, should interfere in the lives of the native population. By the 1920s violent clashes occurred between Jews and Arabs. Determined to safeguard their land against a massive influx of foreign immigrants, Arab leaders sought to deter the British government from its commitment to Jewry. Aware of the seemingly insoluble problem of Arab–Jewish relations in the Holy Land, the British eventually turned over responsibility of governing the area to the United Nations. Once the UN voted for partition of the country, Arabs in

Palestine and elsewhere attacked the newly created Jewish state. For the Palestinian people and Arabs world-wide, the Zionists are colonial usurpers, committed to colonialist policies.

Although the Palestinian leadership was initially convinced that the only viable solution to the Middle East crisis was for there to be one state, in recent years there has been an acceptance of a two-state solution. As Chapter 6 illustrates, in a series of meetings from the 1970s until the present, representatives of the state of Israel and the Palestinian people have met to discuss the ways in which Palestinian aspirations for statehood could be met. Yet, despite the desire of both Israelis and Palestinians for peace, the Middle East conflict has not been resolved. From the Israeli side, the desire for security has been paramount, whereas Palestinians are determined to establish a country in which Palestinians will have the full rights of statehood. Israelis, they insist, must recognize that Palestinians have rights identical to their own, and that past grievances deserve redress. In this context, they stress that the right of return should exist for Palestinians in the same way as it exists for Jews. Palestinians must have absolutely identical legal, civil and democratic rights and equality of opportunity as Israelis do in their own land.

What then should be done? The aim of this book is to highlight the moral dimensions of the Jewish faith, which can provide a framework for considering this ongoing conflict between Israel and the Arab world. As the Conclusion emphasizes, Jews today need to draw from their religious heritage those ethical elements which can help the Jewish community solve the seemingly insoluble problem of the Middle East. What is now required is for Jews to empower the powerless: after more than a century of bloody conflict, the Palestinian people must have a state of their own. Drawing inspiration from the Exodus narrative and the quest to bring about God's Kingdom on earth, we Jews must wholeheartedly support the peace process. On the threshold of a new century, painful compromises must be made by Jews – as well as by Palestinians – in an effort to find a way forward. Only by joining in common cause with Palestinians who seek liberation and freedom can contemporary Jewry echo the ancient words of Isaiah:

I will rejoice in Jerusalem,
and be glad in my people;
no more shall be heard in it the sound of weeping
and the cry of distress . . .
The wolf and the lamb shall feed together,
the lion shall eat straw like the ox;
and dust shall be the serpent's food.
They shall not hurt or destroy
in all my holy mountain, says the Lord (Isa. 65:19,25)

PART I

A Jewish Theology of Liberation

Confronting the challenges of the Middle East conflict, Jews today need to return to the moral foundations of the faith. As Marc Ellis has noted:

> Prophetic Jewish theology; or a Jewish theology of liberation, seeks to bring to light the hidden and sometimes censored movements of Jewish life. It seeks to express the dissent of those afraid or unable to speak. Ultimately, a Jewish theology of liberation seeks, in concern with others, to weave disparate hopes and aspirations in the very heart of Jewish life.
>
> (Ellis, *Towards a Jewish Theology of Liberation*, p. xx)

Given the centrality of the Israeli–Palestinian conflict in Jewish life, such a theology must now address the issue of Palestinian statehood. Today such a theology of liberation can serve as a catalyst to break through the paralysis currently facing the Jewish community.

Throughout history the Jewish people have been God's suffering servant, yet inspired by a vision of God's reign on earth, they have been able to transcend their own misfortunes in attempting to ameliorate the lot of others. In the contemporary world, where Jews are often comfortable and affluent, the prophetic message of liberation can too easily be forgotten. A Jewish theology of liberation, however, with its focus on the desperate situation of those who are currently in bondage can act as a clarion call to the Jewish community, awakening the people of Israel to their divinely appointed task. Jewish tradition points to God's Kingdom as the goal and hope of humankind, a world in which all peoples and nations shall turn away from iniquity and injustice. This is not hope of bliss in a future life, but the building up of the divine kingdom of truth among all peoples. In this quest, the issue of Palestinian statehood is of vital importance.

Chapter 1
The Kingdom of God

Throughout the history of the nation, Jews have been determined to bring about God's Kingdom on earth. According to tradition, Jews expect a total transformation of the world: the reign of God is understood as a Jewish hope for the reordering of earth life. Through the centuries, ethical concern has been at the core of this quest. Now that the Jewish people are established in their ancestral home, we Jews are morally obliged to look beyond the borders of the Jewish state to those who are still in exile.

The Kingdom of God in the Hebrew Bible

In Scripture, the Kingdom of God is understood as intimately connected with the establishment of justice on earth. In the Psalms, for example, God is extolled as a king who judges justly: it was he who righted injustice; he is the heavenly king who established and maintains justice on earth:

> But the Lord sits enthroned for ever
> He has established his throne for judgment;
> he judges the world with righteousness;
> he judges the peoples with equity.

The Lord is a stronghold for the oppressed,
a stronghold in times of trouble.
And those who know thy name put their trust in thee,
for Thou, O Lord, has not forsaken those who seek thee.
(Ps. 9:7–10)

This motif of God as the king who rights the wrongs of the world is related to the Israelite legal emphasis on the rights of the orphan, the widow and the resident foreigner. God is the enthroned sovereign who is responsible for the protection of the weak. According to Psalm 82 it is precisely this which makes him God, and it is because the other so-called gods do not right the wrongs of this world that they expose themselves as false deities. Psalm 82 reads:

God has taken his place in the divine council;
in the midst of the gods he holds judgment:
'How long will you judge unjustly
and show partiality to the wicked?
Give justice to the weak and the fatherless;
maintain the right of the afflicted and the destitute.
Rescue the weak and the needy;
deliver them from the hand of the wicked.'

They have neither knowledge nor understanding,
they walk about in darkness;
all the foundations of the earth are shaken.
I say, 'You are gods,
sons of the Most High, all of you;
nevertheless, you shall die like men,
and fall like any prince.'
(Ps. 82:1–7)

God's nature is to be the divine king who acts justly, and Israel is enjoined to be like God. The Lord stands for righteousness and justice; so too must the earthly king act with lovingkindness and equity:

Give the king thy justice, O God,
and thy righteousness to the royal son!

12

> May he judge thy people with righteousness
> and thy poor with justice!
>
> Let the mountains bear prosperity for the people,
> and the hills in righteousness!
> May he defend the cause of the poor of the people,
> give deliverance to the needy,
> and crush the oppressor!
>
> (Ps. 72:1–4)

Ordinary citizens too are called to the justice of God. By keeping God's commandments Israel is to become truly God's child by bringing peace to earth. When the people acted unjustly, the psalmist called them to account:

> Hear, O my people, and I will speak,
> O Israel, I will testify against you.
> I am God, your God . . .
>
> What right have you to recite my statutes,
> or take my covenant on your lips?
> For you hate discipline,
> and you cast my words behind you.
>
> If you see a thief, you are a friend of his;
> and you keep company with adulterers,
> You give your mouth free reign for evil,
> and your tongue frames deceit.
>
> You sit and speak against your brother;
> you slander your own mother's son.
>
> (Ps. 50:7, 16–20)

Here the emphasis is on justice and the grounding of justice in the holy nature of God indicate a theology of human conduct in every respect congruent with the message of the prophets.

The Rabbis and the Kingdom

Through the centuries Jews have steadfastly adhered to the belief that God is a supreme ruler who calls all peoples to join in bringing about the Kingdom of God on earth. As we have seen, this understanding was an essential element of pslamist theology and a central theological motif of the Hebrew Bible. In later rabbinic literature, this vision of the human role in bringing about God's Kingdom was elaborated further. According to the rabbis, the Kingdom of God will take place in this world. It will be established by human obedience to the divine will. The Kingdom of God consists in a complete moral order on earth-the reign of trust, righteousness, and holiness among all nations. The fulfillment of this conception ultimately rests with the coming of the Messiah. Nevertheless, it is the duty of humanity to participate in the creation of a better world in anticipation of messianic redemption. In the words of rabbinic sages: 'Man is a co-worker with God in the work of creation' (Shab. 119b).

According to rabbinic theology, humanity is the centre of creation for it is only human beings among all of God's creatures who can through righteousness make the Kingdom glorious. In rabbinic midrash, the view is expressed that God's Kingdom did not come into operation until human beings were created:

> When the Holy One, blessed be he, consulted the Torah as to the creation of the world, he answered, 'Master of the world, if there be no host, over whom will the King reign, and if there be no peoples praising him, where is the glory of the King?'
>
> (Pirke Rabbi Eliezer, Ch. 3)

Only human beings then can make the Kingdom glorious. God wanted to reign over free agents who are able to act as God's partners in perfecting the world. But God requires obedience to the ways of righteousness and justice:

> You are my lovers and friends. 'You walk in my ways,' God declared to Israel. 'As the Omnipotent is merciful and gracious, long-suffering and abundant in goodness so be ye . . . feeding the hungry, giving drink to the thirsty, clothing the naked, ransoming the captives, and marrying the orphans'.
>
> (Agadoth Shir Hashirm, 18, 61)

14

The idea of the Kingdom was conceived by the rabbis as ethical in character. As Solomon Schechter remarked:

> If, then, the Kingdom of God was thus originally intended to be in the midst of men and for men at large (as represented by Adam), if its first preachers were, like Abraham, ex-heathens, who addressed themselves to heathens, if, again, the essence of their preaching was righteousness and justice, and if, lastly, the Kingdom does not mean a hierarchy, but any form of government conducted on the principles of righteousness, holiness, justice and charitableness, then we may safely maintain that the Kingdom of God, as taught by Judaism in one of its aspects is universal in its aims.
>
> (Schechter, *Aspects of Rabbinic Theology: Major Concepts of the Talmud*, p. 93)

According to the Hebrew scriptures, God's identification with morality is absolute. In the prophetic writings, as we noted, the primacy of ethical behaviour is asserted, and this emphasis continued throughout rabbinic literature. Believing themselves to possess an authentic oral tradition as to the meaning of the Torah, the rabbis expounded and amplified the ethical injunctions in Scripture. Thus throughout rabbinic literature, the rabbis sought to ensure that God's moral precepts are upheld. In this light the Jewish people are acceptable to God only when fulfilling the commandments of the Torah. Hence we read in the midrash:

> It is like a king who said to his wife, 'Deck yourself with all your ornaments that you may be acceptable to me.' So God says to Israel, 'Be distinguished by the commandments that you may be acceptable to me.' As it says, 'Fair art thou, my beloved, when thou art acceptable to me.'
>
> (Sifre Deut., Wa'ethanan, §36fin., f75b)

For the rabbis, morality and religion form a single, inseparable whole. Faith in God entails the obligation to be good, for God has commanded that the people follow divine moral dictates. This view is eloquently illustrated in rabbinic lore:

It happened once that R. Reuben was in Tiberius on the Sabbath, and a philosopher asked him: 'Who is the most hateful man in the world?' He replied, 'The man who denies his Creator.' 'How so?' said the philosopher. R. Reuben answered, 'Honour thy father and thy mother, thou shalt do no murder, thou shalt not commit adultery, thou shalt not steal, thou shalt not bear false witness against thy neighbour, thou shalt not covet.' No man denies the derivative (i.e. the separate commandments) until he has previously denied the Root (i.e. God), and no man sins unless he has denied him who commanded him not to commit that sin.

(T. Shebu'ot III, 6)

Jewish Moral Principles

Moral precepts are grounded in the will of God. In this light the Torah serves as the blueprint for moral action, and it is through the admonitions of the rabbis in midrashic and Talmudic sources that the Jewish people are encouraged to put the teachings of the Law into effect in their everyday life. In the hierarchy of values, the rabbis declared that justice is of fundamental importance. R. Simeon b. Gamliel, for example, remarked: 'Do not sneer at justice, for it is one of the three feet of the world, for the sages taught that the world stands on three things: justice, truth and peace' (Deut. R. Shofetim, V, 1 and 3). According to R. Elazar:

the whole Torah depends upon justice. Therefore God gave enactments about justice (Exod. 21:1) immediately after the Ten Commandments, because men transgress justice, and God punishes them, and he teaches the inhabitants of the world. Sodom was not overthrown till the men of Sodom neglected justice, and the men of Jerusalem were not banished till they disregarded justice (Ezek. 16:49; Isa. 1:23).

(Ex. R., Mishpatim, 30, 19)

In explaining what is entailed in the principle of justice, the rabbis explained what is required in a court of law. With reference to the Deuteronomic injunction 'thou shalt not take a bribe, for a bribe blinds the eyes of the wise' (Deut. 16:19), R. Hama b. Osa'ya stated:

> If a man suffers from his eyes, he pays much money to a doctor, but it is doubtful whether he will be healed or not. But he who takes a bribe, overturns justice, blinds the eyes, brings Israel into exile and hunger into the world.
>
> (Tanh B. Shofetim, 15b fin.)

Regarding the statement 'In righteousness shall thou judge thy neighbour' (Lev. 19:15), the Sifra proclaims:

> You must not let one litigant speak as much as he wants, and then say to the other 'shorten thy speech'. You must not let one stand and the other sit.
>
> (Sifra, 89a)

Simeon b. Shetach said:

> When you are judging, and there come before you two men, of whom one is rich and the other poor, do not say, 'the poor man's words are to be believed, but not the rich man's.' But just as you listen to the words of the poor man, listen to the words of the rich man, for it is said, 'Ye shall not respect persons in judgment' (Deut. 1:17).
>
> (Ab. R. N. (vers II), XX, 22a)

Like justice, charity is viewed as an essential virtue. The Talmud declares: 'He who gives alms in secret is greater than Moses' (Bab. B., 9b). In another Talmudic passage R. Elazar stated:

> Almsgiving is greater than all sacrifice for it says, 'To give allms is more acceptable to God than sacrifices' (Prov. 21:3). But loving deeds are greater than almsgiving, as it says, 'Sow in almsgiving, reap in love' (Hos. 10:12). Of his sowing a man may eat or no; of his reaping, he will eat assuredly. And he said: 'Almsgiving becomes increasingly perfect according to the amount of love that is shown in it.
>
> (Suk, 49b)

According to the midrash on the Psalms, the gates of the Lord are open to one who cares for others:

> In the future world, man will be asked, 'What was your occupation?' If he replies, 'I fed the hungry,' then they reply, 'This is the gate of the Lord; he who feeds the hungry, let him enter' (Ps. 118:20). So with giving drink to the thirsty, clothing to the naked, with those who look after orphans, and with those, generally, who do deeds of lovingkindness. All these are gates of the Lord, and those who do such deeds shall enter within them.
>
> (Midr. Ps., 118:19)

Hospitality was also considered a cardinal virtue. In a commentary on Exodus, we read:

> God said to Moses, 'I will send thee to Pharaoh.' Moses answered, 'Lord of the world, I cannot; for Jethro has received me, and opened his house to me, so that I am as a son with him. Jethro has received me, and has honourably entertained me; can I depart without his leave?' Hence it says, 'Moses went and returned to Jethro his father-in-law'.
>
> (Tanh, Shemot, §16, f87a)

> Great is hospitality, the rabbis decreed, 'greater even than early attendance at the House of Study or than the reception of the Shekhinah (God's presence)'.
>
> (Sab, 127a)

The Nature of Jewish Ethics

These few examples indicate that the Kingdom of God is inconsistent with injustice and social misery. The effort to bring about the perfection of the world so that God will reign in majesty is a human responsibility. Jewish ethics as enshrined in the Bible and in rabbinic literature is inextricably related to the coming of God's Kingdom. In this context a number of distinctive characteristics of Jewish morality are expressed in the Jewish tradition.

First, as we have seen in connection with the prophets, there was an intensity of passion about the moral demands made upon human beings. For sins of personal greed, social inequity and deceit, the prophet in God's name denounced the people and threatened horrific catastrophes. The voice of the prophet was continually charged with agony and agitation. The prophet Habakkuk, for example, declared:

> Woe to him who heaps up what is not his own . . .
> Woe to him who gets evil gain for his house . . .
> For the stone will cry out from the wall,
> And the beam from the woodwork respond.
> Woe to him who builds a town with blood,
> and founds a city on iniquity.
>
> (Hab., 2:6, 9, 11–12)

Such shrill denunciations of iniquity were the result of the prophetic conviction that people must be stirred from their spiritual slumber. As Abraham Heschel wrote: 'The prophet's word is a scream in the night . . . while the world is at ease and asleep, the prophet feels the blast from heaven' (Heschel, *The Prophets*, p. 16).

Second, Jewish ethics requires that each person be treated equally. Biblical and rabbinic sources show a constant concern to eliminate arbitrary distinctions between individuals so as to establish a proper balance between competing claims. On the basis of the biblical view that everyone is created in the image of God, the Torah declares that false and irrelevant distinctions must not be introduced to disqualify human beings from the right to justice. The fatherhood and motherhood of God implies human solidarity. The Torah rejects the idea of different codes of morality for oneself and others, for the great and the humble, for rulers and ruled, for individuals and nations, for private and public citizens. Given this understanding of the equality of all people, the Torah singles out the underprivileged and the defenseless in society for consideration: 'You shall not afflict any widow or fatherless child' (Exod. 22:22). 'Thou shalt not respect the person of the poor nor honour the person of the great' (Lev. 19:15).

Since all of humanity is created in the image of God, Judaism maintains that there is no fundamental difference between Jew and non-Jew: God's ethical demands apply to all. In the midrash we read:

This is the gate of the Lord into which the righteous shall enter: not priest, Levities, or Israelites, but the righteous, though they be non-Jews.

(Sifra, Acharei Mot, 13)

Indeed, according to the Talmud, the righteous non-Jew was accorded a place in the hereafter: 'The pious of all nations have a share in the world to come' (Sanhedrin 105a). In this light, the rabbis emphasized that Jews must treat their non-Jewish neighbours with lovingkindness. One of the most authoritative rabbis of the last century, I. Spektor, declared:

It is well known that the early as well as the later geonim wrote that we must abide by the law of the land and refrain from dealing unjustly with a non-Jew . . . Therefore my brethren, listen to my voice and live. Study in our Torah to love the Almighty and love people regardless of faith or nationality. Follow justice and do righteousness with Jew and non-Jew alike. The people of my community know that I always caution them in my talks and warn them that there is absolutely no difference whether one does evil to a Jew or non-Jew. It is a well-known fact that when people come to me to settle a dispute, I do not differentiate between Jew and non-Jew. For that is the law according to our holy Torah.

(Spektor, 'Nachal Yitzchak', in Spero, *Morality, Halakhah and the Jewish Tradition*, p. 134)

A third characteristic of Jewish morality is its emphasis on human motivation. The Jewish faith is not solely concerned with actions and their consequences, it also demands right intention. The rabbis explained: 'The Merciful One requires the heart' (San. 106b). It is true that Judaism emphasizes the importance of moral action, but the Jewish faith also focuses attention on rightmindedness: inner experiences – motives, feelings, dispositions, and attitudes – are of supreme moral significance. For this reason the rabbis identified a group of negative commandments in the Torah involving thought. The following are representative examples:

Thou shalt not take vengeance, nor bear any grudge against the children of thy people.

(Deut. 15:7)

There are six things which the Lord hateth . . . a heart that deviseth wicked thoughts.

(Prov. 6:16, 18)

Beware that there be not a base thought in thy heart.

(Deut. 15:9)

In the Mishnah the rabbis elaborated on this concern for the human heart:

Rabbi Eliezer said, '. . . be not easily moved to anger'.

(Avot 2:15)

Rabbi Joshua said, 'The evil eye, the evil inclination, and hatred of his fellow creatures drives a man out of the world'.

(Avot 2:15)

Rabbi Levitas of Yavneh said, 'Be exceedingly lowly of spirit'.

(Avot 2:16)

Connnected with right thought is the Jewish emphasis on right speech. Jewish sources insist that individuals are morally responsible for the words they utter. Proverbs declares: 'Death and life are in the power of the tongue' (Prov. 18:21). Evil words spoken about one person by another could arouse hatred and enmity and destroy human relations. The rabbis considered slander to be a particular evil:

Whoever speaks slander is as though he denied the fundamental principle (existence of God). The Holy One, blessed be He, says of such a person who speaks slander, 'I and he cannot dwell together in the world.'

(Pe'ah 15d, Areakh in 15b)

There was also a positive aspect to this emphasis on human speech. Just as the rabbis condemned false utterances, they urged their disciples to offer cheerful greetings (Avot 1:15, 3:16). Anger could be soothed with gentle words and reconciliation could be brought about.

A final aspect of Jewish ethics is its concern for human dignity; Judaism puts a strong emphasis on the respect due to all individuals. This concept is found in various laws in the Torah and was developed by the rabbis who cautioned that one must be careful not to humiliate or embarrass others. The twelfth-century philosopher Maimonides, for example, wrote:

> A man ought to be especially heedful of his behaviour towards widows and orphans, for their souls are exceedingly depressed and their spirits low, even if they are wealthy. How are we to conduct ourselves towards them? One must not speak to them otherwise than tenderly. One must show them unvarying courtesy; not hurt them physically with hard toil nor wound their feelings with harsh speech.
>
> (Hilchot De'ot, 6.10)

The Torah's concern for human dignity even included thieves. Rabbi Yochanan ben Zakai pointed out that according to the Law whoever stole a sheep should pay a fine of four times the value of the sheep. Whoever stole an ox must pay five times its value. Those who stole sheep had to undergo the embarrassment of carrying the sheep off in their arms and the Torah compensated them for this indignity, but those who stole oxen were spared such embarrassment because they could simply lead the ox by its tether (Baba Kamma, 99b).

Summary

These specific qualities of Jewish ethics illustrate its humane orientation to all of God's creatures. Throughout biblical and rabbinic literature, Jews were encouraged to strive for the highest conception of life in which the rule of truth, righteousness, and holiness will be established among humankind. Such a desire is the eternal hope of God's people – a longing for God's Kingdom as expressed in the daily liturgy of the synagogue. For Jews the coming of the Kingdom in which God's heavenly rule will be made manifest is a process in which all human beings have a role. The coming of the Kingdom requires a struggle for the reign of justice and righteousness on earth. The Kingdom is not an internalized, spiritualized, otherworldly concept. Rather it involves human activity in a historical context. The rabbis elaborated the teaching of the Torah about human partnerships with God in bringing about God's rule. The moral life is at the centre of the unfolding of God's plan for humanity. We now stand on the threshold of a new beginning in the Middle East: the Jewish ethical message which has resounded through the ages calls Jews to seek to transform our imperfect world in anticipation of the divine promise of the eschatological fulfillment at the end of time.

Chapter 2
Exodus and Freedom from Oppression

In the Jewish tradition, the Exodus experience is paradigmatic. It remains vital and contemporary. In confronting the conflict in the Middle East, the redemption of the Israelite nation in ancient times provides a basis for political action: it calls the Jewish nation today to awaken to the cry of those who currently live in exile.

The Exodus from Egypt

In Egypt the ancient Israelites were exploited and oppressed. This experience involved a degradation so severe that it caused the people to turn to God for deliverance. The Egyptians overwhelmed the Hebrew slaves with work: they 'made their lives bitter with hard service, in mortar and brick, and in all kinds of work in the field; in all their work they made them serve with rigour' (Exod. 1:14). Such affliction caused the people to cry out to God for liberation. In response God declared:

> I have seen the affliction of my people who are in Egypt, and have heard their cry because of their taskmasters; I know their

sufferings, and I have come down to deliver them out of the hand of the Egyptians.

(Exod. 3:7–8)

Pharaoh rebuked Moses and Aaron when they demanded the freedom of the Israelite nation. 'Why do you take the people away from their work?' he asked. 'Get to your burdens' (Exod. 5:4). Pharaoh's response to the people's request was to intensify their suffering. The same day,

Pharaoh commanded the taskmasters of the people and their foremen: 'You shall no longer give the people straw to make bricks, as heretofore; let them go and gather straw for themselves. But the number of bricks which they made heretofore you shall lay upon them, you shall by no means lessen it'.

(Exod. 5:6–8)

The intensified affliction, however, did not accomplish Pharaoh's aims, and to defuse the impending conflict he granted various concessions. The Israelites refused all his offers, and the dialogue broke off. The confrontation intensified and led finally to the liberation of the enslaved people. If the Hebrews had accepted Pharaoh's concessions, the struggle would not have become increasingly radical and the ancient Israelites would not have gained their freedom.

In the biblical account, God is on the side of the oppressed. If their is a single passage that encapsulates the liberation themes of Scripture, it is the Exodus describing God who takes sides, intervening to free the poor and oppressed. The Book of Exodus declares that God heard the groaning of the people and remembered the covenant with them (Exod. 2:23–25). God took sides with his chosen people, stating that they would be liberated from their oppressors: Moses was to lead them out of bondage (Ex. 3:7–10).

From this act of deliverance Jews have constantly derived a message of hope: if God was on the side of the poor in ancient times, surely he will continue to take sides with the downtrodden in all ages. Repeatedly, as Jews faced persecution, suffering and murder, they derived hope from this account of divine deliverance. Yet, the biblical narrative is not confined to the destiny of the Jewish nation.

The profundity of the Exodus consists in its significance for all – the past holds a promise for those who understand its relevance. Its message applies to all peoples in economic, political, social and cultural bondage.

In this context, Moses plays a crucial role in the process of liberation. He fled to the desert because he had killed an Egyptian. He lived comfortably as a herdsman with his wife, his father-in-law and his flocks. But one day he heard God speak to him out of a bush. 'Moses, Moses,' God cried,

> I have seen the affliction of my people who are in Egypt, and have heard their cry because of their taskmasters; I know their sufferings, and I have come down to deliver them out of the hand of the Egyptians . . . Come I will send you to Pharaoh that you may bring forth my people, the sons of Israel, out of Egypt.
>
> (Exod. 3:7–10)

Here, God – the other – is revealed to Moses. Moses heard God's command: 'Liberate my people out of Egypt.' Established in the totality of daily life, he responded by becoming the liberator of his people. Arguably we too are being summoned by the plea of those who are oppressed in modern society. Like Moses, we must awaken ourselves to God's command. As in ancient times, if we do not listen to those in bondage, we are not hearkening to the divine call.

In the flight from Egypt, the Bible stressed that it was God who led the people. He did not take them out by way of the land of the Philistines, although that was near, but led the people through the wilderness towards the Red Sea 'Lest the people repent when they see war, and return to Egypt' (Exod. 13:17–18). When the Egyptian army attempted to capture the Israelites, God intervened and they were saved (Exod. 14:24–28).

Once Israel had crossed the Red Sea, God sustained the people in their wanderings: God gave them sweet water at Marah (Exod. 15: 22, 25), sent them manna and quail in the desert (Exod. 16:4–36), gave them safe passage through the Transjordan (Num. 21:21–24, Deut. 2:26–37), and delivered the Amorite kings into the hands of the Israelites (Deut. 3:12–17). Not only did God deliver and protect the people, God also led them to their own land where they were no longer oppressed. Before Moses' death, God proclaimed to Joshua: 'I myself will be with you' (Deut. 31:23). God promised to be with Joshua as God was with Moses (Josh. 1:5). The conquest was thus a second stage of God's deliverance, and even the prostitute of Jericho knew that God would take the side of the people as had happened in the past: 'I know that the Lord has given you the land . . . We have heard how the Lord dried up the water of the Red Sea before you when you came out of Egypt' (Josh. 2:9–10).

The Exodus in the Passover Festival

Throughout Jewish history, the experience of the Exodus has been typologically significant. It is a paradigm of divine liberation of the oppressed and persecuted. The Exodus is thus a key element in the self-understanding of the Jewish people. In the biblical period, details of the Exodus were recorded in cultic sayings (Ps. 107:35–38), in Wisdom literature (Ws. 19), and by the prophets (Isa. 63). After the exile the Exodus continued to play a dominant role in the Jewish faith. In particular, the festival of Passover was regarded as crucially important in the religious life of the nation. As Louis Finkelstein noted:

> The Passover celebration commemorates an event which will probably symbolize for all time the essential meaning of freedom, namely the freedom devoted to a purpose. When Israel came forth from bondage, it was not simply to enjoy liberty, but to make of liberty an instrument of service . . . The Israelites alone made the moment of their origin as a people one of permanent self-dedication to the principle of universal freedom as the essential prerequisite for spiritual growth. Hence the event has meaning for all living people.
>
> (Finkelstein, *Haggadah of Passover*, p. i)

The Passover Seder envisages the Exodus experience as a symbol of freedom from oppression, and the whole of the Haggadah is pervaded by the image of God as the Saviour of humankind. For this reason the Passover service begins with an ancient formulaic invitation to those who hunger or are in need to participate in the festival:

> This is the bread of affliction that our fathers ate in the Land of Egypt. All who hunger, let them come and eat: all who are in need, let them come and celebrate the Passover. Now we are here – next year we shall be free men.

Any Jew who sits down to the Passover meal and is oblivious to the call of those who are in want has missed the meaning of the celebration.

During the service the leader displays the unleavened bread to stimulate the curiosity of the youngsters at the meal. It is then the turn of the youngest child to ask about the nature of the Passover festivities. The entire ritual of the Seder hinges on these inquiries. In reply the leader recites the narrative of the Exodus, stressing the themes of liberation and freedom from oppression:

> We were Pharaoh's henchmen in Egypt; and the Lord our God brought us out thereof with a mighty hand and an outstretched arm. Now, had not the Holy One brought our fathers from Egypt, then we and our children and our children's children would be enslaved to Pharaoh in Egypt. Wherefore, even were we all wise men, all men of understanding, all advanced in years, all men with knowledge of the Torah, it would yet be our duty to recount the story of the coming forth from Egypt; and all who recount at length the story of the coming forth from Egypt are verily to be praised.

This response, based on Deut. 6:21, implies that Passover does not simply commemorate a triumph of remote antiquity. Rather, the Passover ceremony is a celebration of the emancipation of each Jew in every generation, for had it not been for the Exodus Jews would still be slaves in Egypt. Historical continuity is at the heart of this understanding, and is illustrated further by the response made to the wicked son who asks, 'What mean ye by this service?' The leader responds:

> He infers 'ye'; not himself. By shutting himself off from the general body, it is as though he denies the existence of God. Therefore thou shouldst distress him too, replying: 'This is

done because of that which the Lord did unto me when I came forth out of Egypt' – Unto me, not him; for if he had been there he would not have been delivered.

The keynote of the Haggadah is enshrined in a central pledge of the Seder:

It is this Divine pledge that has stood by our fathers and by us also. Not only one man hath risen against us to destroy us, but in every generation men have risen against us to destroy us: But the Holy One delivereth us always from their hand.

Here, Pharaoh's action is seen as a paradigm of all attempts by Israel's enemies to persecute the Jewish people. Echoes of centuries of persecution are evoked by these words, yet it is made clear that God has been and will continue to be on the side of oppressed people. In the symbols of the Passover meal, deliverance is re-enacted. Explaining this symbolism, the leader states with regard to the shankbone of the lamb:

The Passover Lamb that our fathers used to eat when the Temple was still standing – that was because the Holy One, Blessed be He, passed over the house of our fathers in Egypt, as it is said: 'Ye shall say, It is the sacrifice of the Lord's Passover, who passed over the houses of the children of Israel in Egypt, when he smote the Egyptians and delivered our houses.' And the people bowed the head and worshipped.

The unleavened bread is the bread of affliction, the historical emblem of the Exodus. The leader declares it is the symbol of sympathy for the enslaved as well as that of freedom from oppression:

This unleavened bread that we eat – what is the reason? It is because there was no time for our ancestors' dough to become leavened, before the King, King of all Kings, the Holy One, revealed himself to them and redeemed them, as it is said: 'And they baked unleavened cakes of the dough which they brought forth out of Egypt, for it was not leavened: because they were thrust out of Egypt, and could not tarry, neither had they prepared for themselves any victual.'

The bitter herbs, the symbol of bitterness and servitude, remind the Jews that it is their duty as descendants of slaves to lighten the stranger's burden:

> This bitter herb that we eat – what is its reason? It is because the Egyptians embittered the life of our ancestors in Egypt, as it is said: 'And they made their lives bitter with hard bondage, in mortar and brick, and in all manner of service in the field, all their service, when they made them serve, was with rigour.'

The lesson of the Passover service – deeply engraved on the hearts of the Jewish nation – is that persecution and divine deliverance are realities of the present as well as the past. In each generation, Jews must think of themselves as delivered from a perpetual enemy and should assume the responsibility of rescuing those who suffer under oppression. 'In each and every generation,' the Haggadah states,

> it is a man's duty to regard himself as though he went forth out of Egypt, as it is said, 'And thou shalt tell thy son in that day saying, This is done because of that which the Lord did unto me when I came forth out of Egypt.' Not our fathers only did the Holy One redeem, but us too he redeemed, as it is said, 'And he brought us out from thence, that he might bring us in, to give us the land which he swore unto our fathers'.

The Passover in Rabbinic Literature

The Passover celebration is thus a symbolic exaltation of freedom. Jews are all to rejoice in God's liberation of their ancestors, in which each of them takes part. Throughout the history of the Jewish people this festival has awakened the spirit of the people to the significance of human liberation. The biblical account of the Exodus, embodied in the liturgy of the Haggadah, has played a central role in the Jewish quest for human dignity and freedom. When we turn to the Passover in post-biblical literature, we find that Jewish writers also saw in the Exodus a source of hope and inspiration, even during the darkest hours of Jewish history. The lessons of the Haggadah were taught repeatedly by Jewish sages in the midrash and Talmud through commentary, interpretation and legend; in this way new meanings were added to the biblical account.

In Midrash Shemot Rabbah, for example, the rabbis explained why Moses was chosen to lead the Hebrews out of Egypt:

> Our rabbis said that when Moses our teacher, peace be upon him, was tending the flock of Jethro in the wilderness, a little kid escaped from him. He ran after it until it reached a shady place. When it reached the shady place, there appeared to view a pool of water and the kid stopped to drink. When Moses approached it, he said: 'I did not know that you ran away because of thirst; you must be weary.' So he placed the kid on his shoulder and walked away. Thereupon God said, 'Because you have mercy in leading the flock of an animal, you will assuredly tend my flock Israel'.
>
> (Midrash Shemot Rabbah, 2.2)

In the Pirke de-Rabbi Eliezer, the rabbis emphasized the symbolic significance of the burning bush. Commenting on Exodus 3:2, they asked why God showed Moses a bush burning with fire. The reason, they maintained, was because Moses had thought to himself that the Egyptians might consume Israel. Hence God showed him a fire that burnt but was not consumed, saying to him, 'Just as the thorn-bush is burning and is not consumed, so the Egyptians will not be able to destroy Israel' (Pirke de-Rabbi Eliezer, 40).

Similarly, when Moses asked God for a sign, the Lord told him to cast his staff to the ground, and it became a fiery serpent. This was done to illustrate that as the serpent bites and kills human beings, so Pharaoh and his people bit and slew the Israelites (Pirke de Rabbi Eliezer, 40). Moses' hand became leprous in order to show that as the leper is unclean and causes uncleanliness, so Pharaoh and his people were unclean and they caused Israel to be unclean. Later, however, Moses became clean again and God declared: 'Likewise Israel shall become clean from the uncleanliness of the Egyptians' (Pirke de-Rabbi Eliezer, 40).

The rabbis emphasized that the God of the Israelites, unlike the gods of other nations, is the God of the living not the God of the dead. Thus, when Moses and Aaron stood before Pharaoh, they said to him: 'We are the ambassadors of the Lord.' When he heard their request, Pharaoh became very angry and said: 'Who is the Lord that I should hearken unto his voice to let Israel go' (Exod. 5:2). He then went into his palace chamber and scrutinized every nation and its gods. He then said to them, 'I have searched for his name throughout my archives, but have not found him.' Moses and Aaron then said to Pharaoh, 'Idiot! Is it the way of the dead to be sought for among the living, or are the living among the dead? Our God is living, whereas those you mentioned are dead' (Midrash Shemot Rabbah, 4.14).

The rabbis were anxious to point out that God was not responsible for Pharaoh's actions even though Scripture states that God hardened Pharaoh's heart (Exod. 10:1). Simon b. Lakish declared:

> Let the mouths of the heretics be stopped up . . . When God warns a man once, twice, and even a third time, and he still does not repent, then does God close his heart against repentance so that he should exact vengeance from him for his sins. Thus it was with the wicked Pharaoh. Since God sent five times to him and he took no notice, God then said, 'You have stiffened your neck and hardened your heart; well, I will add to your uncleanness!'
>
> (Midrash Shemot Rabbah, 13:3)

Yet despite this action, the rabbis emphasized that God does not rejoice in the downfall of the wicked. R. Johanan asked, 'What is the meaning of the verse, "And one came not near the other all the night" (Exod. 14:20)? The ministering angels wanted to chant their hymns, but the Holy One, blessed be he, said, "The work of my hands is being drowned in the sea, and shall you chant hymns?"' (Megillah, 10b).

The Passover in Later Judaism

Just as rabbinic sources of the Tannaitic and Amoraic periods frequently allude to the Exodus event as central in the life of the

Jewish nation, so in Jewish literature of the medieval period there were frequent references of this act of deliverance. Judah Halevi explained why the liturgy stated that the prohibition of work on the Sabbath and on holy days was a remembrance of the departure from Egypt. These two things belonged together, he wrote, because they were the outcome of the absolute divine will. Quoting Deuteronomy 4:32–34 he asserted:

> For ask now of the days past . . . whether there hath been any such things as this great thing, or hath been heard like it. Did ever people hear the voice of God speaking out of the midst of the fire, as thou hast heard, and live? Or hath God assayed to go and take him a nation from the midst of another nation, by trials, by signs, and by wonders, and by war, and by a mighty hand, and by an outstretched arm, and by great terrors, according to all that the Lord, your God did for you in Egypt before thine eyes?
>
> (Halevi, *The Kuzari*, p. 114)

The medieval Jewish philosopher Saadiah Gaon, in *The Book of Doctrines and Beliefs*, argued that the redemption from bondage was inevitable. God, he maintained, was just and would not do wrong. Having inflicted on the Jewish people prolonged suffering as a punishment, God set a time limit to their affliction. 'Bid Jerusalem take heart and proclaim unto her that her time of service is accomplished, that her guilt is paid off, that she hath received of the Lord's hand double for all her sins' (Isa. 40:2).

Furthermore, God was a faithful keeper of promises; thus the promise that God would mete out judgment to the oppressors of the Jews and reward the Hebrew nation was certain to be fulfilled: 'And also that nation whom they shall serve, will I judge; and afterwards, they shall come out with great substance' (Gen. 15:14). For the trials of the past God would give the people a double of its double share – over and above what had been promised. Thus it was said, 'And he will do thee good and multiply thee above thy fathers' (Deut. 30:5). For this reason Saadiah asserted:

> He mentions to us the Exodus from Egypt so frequently and in so many places. He wants us to remember the things we

experienced. If anything which he did for us in the course of the redemption from Egypt is not explicitly included in the promise of the final Redemption, it is implied in the statement, 'As in the days of thy coming forth out of the land of Egypt, will I show unto him marvelous things' (Micah, 7:15).

(Gaon, *The Book of Doctrines and Beliefs*, pp. 168–169)

The Zohar, the medieval mystical book, relates that the joy of the Passover caused God to rejoice and call together all the heavenly hosts and say to them:

'Come ye and hearken unto the praises which my children bring unto me. Behold how they rejoice in redemption!' Then all the angels gathered together and observed Israel's singing because of God's redemption. Seeing this they also broke into rejoicing that God possessed such a people whose joy in the redemption was so great and powerful. For all that terrestrial rejoicing increased the power of the Lord and his hosts in the regions above, just as an earthly king gained strength from the praises of his subjects, the fame of his glory being thus spread throughout the world.

(Zohar, 'Ray'a Mehamna,' BO, 40b)

Modern Jewish writers of post-Enlightenment Judaism similarly emphasized the significance of the themes of liberty, redemption and freedom as found in the Passover festival. Franz Rosenzweig, for example, argued that there is an intrinsic connection between the Passover and the Sabbath. The Sabbath, he maintained, is a reminder of the Exodus from Egypt:

The freedom of the man-servant and the maid-servant which it proclaims is conditioned by the deliverance of the people as a people from the servitude of Egypt. And in every command to respect the freedom of even the man-servant, of even the alien among the people, the law of God renews the awareness of the connection holding between the freedom within the people, a freedom decreed by God, and the freeing of the people from Egyptian servitude, a liberation enacted by God.

(Rosenzweig, *The Star of Redemption*, pp. 319–321)

The Passover meal was a symbol of Israel's vocation as a people; the deliverance of the nation afforded a glimpse of its destiny. It was not only then that enemies rose up against the Jews; enemies have arisen in every generation, and God has always taken the side of his chosen people. All this pointed to the ultimate redemption as prophesied by Isaiah – of the day when the wolf would dwell with the lamb and the world would be as full of the knowledge of the Lord as the sea is of water (Rosenzweig, *The Star of Redemption*, pp. 319–321).

The moral implications of the redemption from Egypt were emphasized by M. Lazarus in *The Ethics of Judaism*. The Exodus, he wrote, had a predominant place in the biblical and rabbinic cycle of religious ideas. The most exalted moral statutes in the Torah concerning the treatment of strangers were connected with the Exodus, and were, from a psychological point of view, impressively elucidated by means of the injunction: 'Ye know the heart of the stranger' (Exodus 23:9). The prophets and the psalmists used this event to illustrate God's providence and grace, and the rabbis deduced from it the two fundamental aspects of Jewish ethics: the notion of liberty and the ethical task of humankind. Throughout the history of Judaism, Lazarus remarked,

> The notion of liberty, inner moral and spiritual liberty, cherished as a pure, exalted ideal, possible only under and through the Law, was associated with the memory of the redemption from Egyptian slavery, and this memory in turn was connected with symbolic practices accompanying every act, pleasure, and celebration.
>
> (Lazarus, *The Ethics of Judaism*, pp. 28–29, 231–232)

Kaufmann Kohler saw in the Passover a symbol of thanksgiving and hope that sustained the Jewish nation in its tribulations:

> The Passover festival with its 'night of divine watching' endowed the Jew ever anew with endurance during the dark night of medieval tyranny and with faith in 'the Keeper of Israel who slumbereth not nor sleepeth'.
>
> (Kohler, *Jewish Theology*, p. 462)

Moreover, he believed that the feast of redemption promised a day of liberty to those who continue to struggle under oppression and exploitation:

> The modern Jew is beginning to see in the reawakening of his religious and social life in Western lands the token of the future liberation of all mankind. The Passover feast brings him the clear and hopeful message of freedom for humanity from all bondage of today and of spirit.
>
> (Kohler, *Jewish Theology*, p. 462)

M. Joseph also focused on the contemporary significance of Passover in *Judaism as Creed and Life*. It is, he wrote, the greatest of all the historical festivals in that it brings the Jews into close contact with the past. No other festival, he argued, so powerfully appeals to historic sympathies. At the Passover ceremony the Jews are at one with their redeemed ancestors; they share with the ancestors the consciousness of freedom, the sense of nationality that was beginning to stir in their hearts. 'He [the Jew] shares,' Joseph wrote, 'their glowing hopes, the sweet joy of newly recovered manhood' (Joseph, *Judaism as Creed and Life*, pp. 213–215).

Through God's redemption the Israelites were able to free themselves from despair, and all Jews, past and present, share in this deliverance.

> We march forth with them from the scenes of oppression in gladness and gratitude. The ideal of the rabbis fulfils itself. 'In every generation it is for the Jew to think that he himself forth from Egypt' (Pesahim, 10:5).
>
> (Joseph, *Judaism as Creed and Life*, pp. 213–215)

Ahad Ha-Am concentrated on Moses the Liberator as an ideal type of hero. Moses, he pointed out, was neither a warrior nor a statesman. He was a prophet, who put justice into action. Confronted with acts of iniquity, he took the side of the victim. The events of his early life, when he struggled against injustice, served as a prelude to his revolt against Egyptian oppression:

That great moment dawned in the wilderness, far from the tur-
moil of life. The prophet's soul is weary of the endless struggle, and longs for peace and rest. He seeks the solitude of the
shepherd's life, goes into the wilderness with his sheep, and
reaches Horeb, the mountain of the Lord. But even here he
finds no rest. He feels in his innermost being that he has not yet
fulfilled his mission . . . Suddenly the prophet hears the voice
of the Lord – the voice he knows so well – calling to him from
some forgotten corner of his innermost being: 'I am the God of
thy father . . . I have surely seen the affliction of my people that
are in Egypt . . . Come now therefore, and I will send thee unto
Pharaoh, that thou mayest bring forth my people the children
of Israel out of Egypt'.

(Ahad Ha-Am, *Essays, Letters, Memoirs*, pp. 103–108)

In the modern period Jewish poets have also celebrated the message
of liberation. Even in the Warsaw Ghetto, Passover had the power
to move the hearts of those who endured suffering and death:

Pesach has come to the ghetto again,
The wine has no grape, the matzah no grain,
But the people anew sing the wonders of old,
The flight from the Pharaohs, so often retold.
How ancient the story, how old the refrain!

The windows are shuttered. The doors are concealed.
The Seder goes on. And fiction and fact
Are confused into one. Which is myth? Which real?
'Come all who are hungry!' invites the Haggadah.
The helpless, the aged, lie starving in fear.
'Come all who are hungry!' and children sleep, famished.
'Come all who are hungry!' and tables are bare.

Pesach has come to the ghetto again,
And shuffling shadows shift stealthily through,
Seeking a retreat with the God of the Jews.
But these are the shards, the shattered remains
Of the 'sixty-ten-thousands' whom Moses led out

Of their bondage . . . driven to ghettos again . . .
Where dying's permitted but protest is not.
From Holland, from Poland, from all Europe's soil,
And there they sit weeping, plundered, despoiled,
And each fifty families has dwindled to one.

Pesach has come to the ghetto again.
The lore-laden words of the Seder are said,
And the cup of the prophet Elijah awaits,
But the Angel of Death has intruded, instead.
As always – the German snarls his commands.
As always – the words sharpened-up and precise.
As always – the fate of more Jews in his hands:
Who shall live, who shall die, this Passover night.
But no more will the Jews to the slaughter be led.
The truculent jibes of the Nazis are past.
And the lintels and doorposts tonight will be red
With the blood of free Jews who will fight to the last.
(Goodman, *The Passover Anthology*, pp. 264–265)

Summary

Reflecting on the significance of Passover, it is clear that Jews have found renewed strength and hope in the message of the Exodus. The Passover ceremony unites the Jewish people with their ancestors who endured slavery and oppression in Egyptian bondage. Despite the persecution of centuries, the Jewish nation is confident of eventual deliverance and the ultimate redemption of humankind. The message of the Exodus calls the Jewish people to hold steadfast to their conviction that justice and freedom will prevail throughout the world. Jews thus possess a biblical heritage and vision of the transformation of society, and the Exodus event unites them in a common hope and aspiration for the triumph of justice. Remembering the divine deliverance of the ancient Israelites, Jews in Israel and the diaspora can work together for the emancipation of those Palestinians who long to escape from exile.

Chapter 3
Theology and Praxis

For the Jewish people, moral values are at the heart of the tradition. In the unfolding narrative of the Jewish nation in Scripture, ethical commands predominate. The Jewish people are to be a light to all nations, bringing God's message of truth and justice to the world.

History and Praxis

As we have seen, the Exodus was the central salvific event in the history of ancient Israel. The reign of the Pharaoh was oppressive. In response God chose to create a nation of free human beings. The process of liberation began with violence. First Moses – upset by the cruelty of the Egyptian taskmasters – killed an Egyptian (Exod. 2:12). Following this act of rebellion, a violent struggle ensued. The first-born of the Egyptians died (Exod. 12:29–30), and God eventually prevailed when the waters drowned the Egyptian host.

Experiencing the redeeming power of their Lord, the Israelites burst into a song of thanksgiving celebrating God's defeat of their oppressors:

> I will sing to the lord, for he has triumphed gloriously;
> the horse and his rider he has thrown into the sea.
> The Lord is my strength and my song,

and he has become my salvation;
this is my God, and I will praise him,
my father's God, and I will exalt him.
The Lord is a man of war; the Lord is his name.
Pharaoh's chariots and his host he has cast into the sea;
and his picked officers are sunk in the Red Sea.
The floods cover them;
they went down into the depths like a stone.
Thy right hand, O Lord, glorious in power,
thy right hand, O Lord, shatters the enemy.
In the greatness of thy majesty thou overthrowest thy
    adversaries;
thou sendest forth thy fury, it consumes them like a stubble.
At the blast of thy nostrils the waters piled up,
the floods stood up in a heap;
the deeps congealed in the heart of the sea.

(Exod. 15:1–8)

Here we read that God acts with vigour: 'I know that the King of Egypt will not let you go unless compelled by a mighty hand' (Exod. 3:19). If oppression is carried to the extreme of repression, liberation is necessarily violent. God acted violently in the Exodus account because the situation of the ancient Hebrews admitted no other path. At first God sent Moses and Aaron to petition the king to allow their people to go. But the replies of Pharaoh illustrate that the oppressor never liberates. Therefore God turned to violence as a final resort. The demands of love called for a violent act. Why did God act in this way? It is because oppression is never justifiable. Injustice can never be rationalized. Nor is it tolerable through resignation when legal or peaceful means to eradicate it are exhausted. Justice demands of love a violent reaction.

The Bible is thus a record of divine intervention in human history. What was required of Israel was obedient participation in the fulfillment of God's plan of emancipation. The faith of Israel was portrayed as synonymous with acting in consonance with God's will. The biblical witness leads to a historical orientation of the Jewish faith. Praxis, rather than theological conceptualization, serves as the foundation of Jewish commitment and obedience.

A Jewish theology of liberation must start from actions committed to the cause of liberation. Theology is thus conceived as a critical reflection on praxis. Theology and action are inextricably linked. It is a mistake to believe that timeless truths can be applied to a finished universe. Rather, the world and human comprehension are incomplete – each requires refinement and development. Spiritual knowledge is not the conformity of the mind to the given, but an immersion in the process of transformation and construction of a new world.

This process involves a constant interaction of practice and theory. For Jews, such a praxis is a means by which a new heaven and a new earth can be formed. It is transforming action in tension with theory. Praxis grows out of and responds to historical circumstance. Thus theology should be understood as a critical reflection on human activity. Unlike traditional Jewish theology, which was concerned with eternal realities, a Jewish liberation theology is oriented to action. Truth is not defined a priori, independent of historical verification. A theology of liberation insists on a historical basis. Faith can only be historically true when it becomes true, when it is effective in the liberation of the oppressed. In this way the truth dimension of faith is directly linked to its ethical and political dimensions. Such a historically rooted view of theology has serious implications for dealing with the complexities of the Middle East crisis.

Judaism and Moral Action

For Jews, history matters. The Jewish hope for the future lies in God's sovereign rule on earth. From ancient times the synagogue liturgy concluded with a prayer in which this hope is expressed:

> May we speedily behold the glory of thy might,
> when thou wilt remove the abominations from the earth,
> and the idols will be utterly cut off;
> when the world will be perfected under the kingdom of the
>   Almighty,
> and all the children of flesh will call upon thy name;
> when thou wilt turn unto thyself all the wicked of the earth.

This is the goal of the history of the world in which God's chosen people have a central role. In this context the people of Israel have a historical mission to be a light to the nations. Through Moses God addressed the people and declared:

> You have seen what I did to the Egyptians, and how
> I bore you on eagles' wings, and brought you unto myself.
> Now, therefore, if you will obey my voice and keep my covenant,
> you shall be my own possession among all peoples; for all
> the earth is mine, and you shall be to me a kingdom of priests and a holy nation.
>
> (Exod. 19:4–6)

Election was to be a servant of the Lord, to proclaim God's truth and righteousness throughout the world. Being chosen meant duty and responsibility. It was a divine call persisting through all ages and encompassing all lands, a continuous activity of the spirit which has ever summoned for itself new heralds and heroes to testify to truth, justice and sublime faith.

Judaism did not separate religion from life. Instead Jews were called to action, to turn humankind away from violence, wickedness and falsehood. It was not the hope of bliss in a future life but the establishment of the kingdom of justice and peace that was central to the Jewish faith. Moral praxis is at the heart of the religious tradition. The people of Israel as a light to the nations reflects the moral nature of God. Each Jew is to be like the creator, mirroring the divine qualities revealed to Moses: 'The Lord, the Lord, a God merciful and gracious, slow to anger, and abounding in steadfast love and faithfulness, keeping steadfast love for thousands, forgiving iniquity and transgression and sin' (Exod. 34:6–7).

God as a moral being demands moral living as the Psalms declare: 'The Lord is righteous: he loves righteous deeds' (Ps. 11:7). 'Righteousness and justice are the foundation of his throne' (Ps. 97:2). 'Thou has established equity; thou hast executed justice and righteousness' (Ps. 99:4). Given this theological framework, Jews were directed to obey the revealed will of God, which is the basis of the covenantal relationship between God and the Jewish nation.

Orthopraxis, rather than conceptual reflection, serves as the foundation of the religion of Israel.

In the Bible, deeds and events involving moral issues can be found in abundance: the punishment of Cain for murdering his brother; the violence of the generation that brought on the flood; the early prohibition against murder; the hospitality of Abraham and his pleading for the people of Sodom; the praise of Abraham for his moral attitudes; the condemnation of Joseph's brothers; Joseph's self-restrain in the house of Potiphar; Moses intercessions on the side of the exploited.

But it is preeminently in the legal codes of the Torah that we encounter moral guidelines formulated in specific rules. The Decalogue in particular illustrates the centrality of moral praxis in the life of the Jew. The first four commandments are theological in character, but the last six deal with relationships between human beings. The first commandment describes God as the one who redeemed the Jews from Egypt; the one who forbade the worship of other deities and demanded respect for the Sabbath and the divine name. These commandments are expressions of the love and fear of God; the remaining injunctions provide a means of expressing love of other human beings. The Decalogue makes it clear that moral rules are fundamental to Judaism.

Such ethical standards are repeated in the prophetic books. The teachings of the prophets are rooted in the Torah of Moses. The prophets saw themselves as messengers of the divine word. Their special task was to denounce the people for their transgressions and call them to repentance. In all this they pointed to concrete action – moral praxis – as the only means of sustaining the covenantal relationship with God. The essential theme of their message is that God demands righteousness and justice.

Emphasis on the moral life is reflected in the prophetic condemnation of cultic practices that are not accompanied by ethical concern. These passages illustrate that ritual commandments are of instrumental value. Morality is intrinsic and absolute. The primacy of morality is also reflected in the prophetic warning that righteous action is the determining factor in the destiny of the Jewish nation. Moral transgressions referred to in such contexts concern exploitation, oppression and the perversion of justice. These sins have the potential to bring about the downfall of the nation.

The Book of Proverbs reinforces the teaching of the Torah and the prophets. Wisdom is conceived here as the capacity to act morally; it is a skill that can be learned. Throughout Proverbs dispositional traits are catalogued. The positive moral types include the *tzaddik*, the *chakham*, and the *yashar*; the evil characters include the *rasha*, the *avil*, the *kheseil*, the *letz* and the *peti*. This suggests that moral virtue and vice is to be achieved not by concentrating on individual moral acts but rather by learning to recognize and emulate certain good personality types. Thus, here, as in the rest of the Bible, the moral life was seen as the foundation of the Jewish faith. Theology is defined in relation to practical activity. It is through ethical praxis that humanity encounters the Divine.

Rabbinic literature continued this emphasis on action. Convinced that they were the authentic expositors of Scripture, the rabbis amplified biblical law. In their expansion of the commandments, rabbinic exegetes differentiated between the laws governing human relationships to God and those that concern human relationships to others. As in the biblical period, rabbinic teachings reflect the same sense of the primacy of morality. Such texts as the following indicate rabbinic priority:

> He who acts honestly and is popular with his fellow creatures, it is imputed to him as though he had fulfilled the entire Torah.
> Hillel said: 'What is hateful to yourself, do not do to your fellow man. This is the entire Torah, the rest is commentary.'
> Better is one hour of repentance and good deeds in this world than in the whole life of the world-to-come.
> (Spero, *Morality, Halakhah and the Jewish Tradition*, pp. 56–57)

In the classic texts of Judaism, then, moral behaviour is the predominant theme. By choosing the moral life, the Jew is able to help complete God's work of creation. To accomplish this task the rabbis formulated an elaborate system of traditions, which were written down in the Mishnah, subsequently expanded in the Talmud, and eventually codified in the Code of Jewish Law. According to traditional Judaism, this expansion of Pentateuchal Law is part of

God's revelation. Both the Written Law (*Torah Shebikthav*) and the Oral Law (*Torah Shebe'alpe*) are binding on Jews for all time.

This Torah embraces the Pentateuch as well as its traditional interpretation: Orthodoxy maintains that God gave to Moses the laws in the Pentateuch as well as their explanations:

> The verse: 'And I will give thee the tables of stone, and the Law and the commandment, which I have written that thou may-est teach them' (Exod. 24:12) means as follows: 'The tables of stone' are the ten commandments. 'The law' is the Pentae-uch. 'The commandment' is the Mishnah; 'which have writ-ten' are the Prophets and the Hagiographa'; 'that thou mayest teach them' is the Gemara (Talmud). This teaches that all these things were given on Sinai (R. Levi b. Hamma in the name of R. Simeon b. Laquish).

Given this view of the Torah, Jews regarded the moral law as abso-lute and binding. In all cases the law was precise and specific; it was God's word made concrete in the daily life of the Jew. The command-ment to love one's neighbours embraced all humanity. In the Code of Jewish Law the virtues of justice, honesty and humane concern were regarded as central virtues of community life; hatred, venge-ance, deceit, cruelty and anger were condemned as antisocial. The Jew was instructed to exercise loving kindness towards all; to clothe the naked, to feed the hungry, to care for the sick, and to comfort the mourner. By fulfilling these ethical demands, the Jewish people could help to bring about God's Kingdom on earth, in which exploitation, oppression and injustice would be eliminated. What is required in this task is a commitment to ethical praxis.

Orthopraxis versus Orthodoxy

In contrast to this emphasis on the centrality of moral praxis, the Jewish religion does not insist on the acceptance of formal theo-logical dogma. The hallmark of the Jewish tradition is orthopraxis rather than theological orthodoxy. In the history of the Jewish faith there has never been a central body that took upon itself the respon-sibility of formulating a religious creed. The books of the Bible and early rabbinic literature contain numerous beliefs about God's nature and activity, yet neither the Bible nor the Mishnah contains a list of correct beliefs nor a commandment to believe in God. It was not until the Hellenistic period that there was an attempt to outline the articles of the Jewish faith.

Responding to contemporary views that he believed to be against the spirit of the Jewish faith, the first-century philosopher Philo formulated five principles that he felt Jews were bound to accept: God is eternal; God is one; the world was created; the world is one; God exercises forethought. It is noteworthy that these beliefs were conditioned by external circumstances. Philo did not examine the sources of Judaism in an objective manner to discover the basic principles of the faith; his purpose was simply to highlight the ideas that needed to be stressed as principles of the faith in his time in response to the external challenge to Jewish belief.

Only infrequently in the development of early rabbinic Judaism were there other attempts to categorize the essential principles of Judaism. Significantly, such lists included action as well as belief. For the rabbis it is impossible to separate religious conviction from ethical demands. In the third century, for example, Rabbi Simlai declared that the Torah could be reduced to a number of principles as reflected in the teachings of various biblical personages. King David, he maintained, summarized the Torah in eleven essentials:

 (1) He who walks blamelessly
 (2) and does what is right
 (3) and speaks truth from his heart
 (4) and does not slander with his tongue,
 (5) and does no evil to his friend,
 (6) nor takes up a reproach against his neighbour
 (7) in whose eyes a reprobate is despised,
 (8) but who honors those who fear the Lord
 (9) who swears to his own hurt and does not change,
(10) who does not put out his money at interest,
(11) and does not take a bribe against the innocent (Ps. 15:2–5).

Isaiah reduced the Torah to six principles:

(1) He who walks righteously
(2) and speaks uprightly
(3) who despises the gain of oppressions
(4) who shakes his hands, lest they hold a bribe
(5) who stops up his ears from hearing of bloodshed
(6) and shuts his eyes from looking upon evil (Isa. 33:15).

Micah reduced it to two principles:

(1) To do justice to love kindness,
(2) and to walk humbly with thy God (Micah 6:8).

Amos reduced it to one:

(1) Seek me and live (Amos 5:4).

As did Habakkuk:

(1) But the righteous shall live by his faith (Hab. 2:4).

We can see that belief and action were inextricably interrelated. For Rabbi Simlai – as for others – the essence of Judaism lay in the practical expression of the Jews' adherence to God's moral demands.

It was not until the Middle Ages, when Jewish scholars faced the challenge of Greek philosophical thought as well as Christianity and Islam, that they again felt it necessary to outline the essential theological features of their faith. As with Philo, the rabbis of this period attempted to defend Judaism and to dwell on what they perceived as its unique features in order to combat an external threat. The most important formulation was Maimonides' thirteen principles of the Jewish faith. Here, as in Philo's list, the emphasis was on correct belief; only those who subscribe to these tenets are to be included in the general body of Israel.

Other Jewish thinkers challenged Maimonides' formulation. Hasdai Crescas, for example, maintained that there is one basic belief, eight other important beliefs, eleven true opinions, and thirteen probabilities. Simon ben Zemah Duran argued that there are only three essential principles of the Jewish faith, which include by implication Maimonides' other principles. Similarly, Joseph Albo declared that there are three principles, eight derived beliefs, and six tenets, which everyone professing the Law of Moses is obliged to believe. Other scholars insisted that it is impossible to extract a set of principles from the Torah. Asked whether he accepted the formulations of Maimonides, Crescas or Albo, David ben Solomon Ibn Abi Zimra stated: 'I do not agree that it is right to make any part of the perfect Torah into a "principle" since the whole Torah is a "principle" from the Mouth of the Almighty.'

It was not surprising that there was such disagreement among rabbinic authorities since the classic texts of Judaism are essentially nonspeculative in character. Without an overall authority whose opinion in theological matters is binding on all Jews, it was inevitable that rabbinic opinion would conflict about such a central issue as the fundamental tenets of the faith. And without such a binding framework of religious belief, equally contentious discussions often arose over theological matters.

A major religious disagreement divided the Jewish community as early as the Hellenistic period. The Sadducees adhered to the literal meaning of the Pentateuch and rejected the belief in an afterlife, whereas the Pharisees believed that the soul survived death and that God revealed the Oral as well as the Written Law. According to Josephus, the Pharisees believed that souls have power to survive death and that there are rewards and punishments under the earth for those who have led lives of virtue or vice. The Sadduccees hold that the soul perishes along with the body. They own no observances of any sort apart from the laws.

Theological Debate and Later Judaism

In later Judaism, Jewish thinkers continued to differ about fundamental matters. Maimonides argued that God should only be described by using negative attributes; to ascribe to God positive attributes, he believed, is a form of polytheism because it suggests that other beings, namely the divine attributes, are coexistent with God for all eternity. According to Maimonides, when we declare that God is one, we are not saying anything about God's true nature, but we are negating all plurality from the divine being.

Positive attributes are permitted only if it is understood that they refer to God's actions rather than his nature.

Hasdai Crescas disputed this claim. It is impossible, he contended, to avoid the use of positive attributes, and there is nothing offensive in using them since there is a real relationship between God and the world he created, even though God is infinite and creatures finite. Another theory was put forward by the kabbalists who distinguished between God as he is in himself and God as manifested to creatures. For the kabbalists, God is revealed through divine emanations, but God as God is the *En Sof*. Positive attributes, they maintained, are permissible in speaking of God as manifest; but of God as God, not even negative attributes are then allowed.

Jewish thinkers also had differing opinions concerning God's omniscience. According to Gersonides and Crescas, it is logically impossible for God to have foreknowledge and for human beings to have free will. For Gersonides, God knows things in general but is not omniscient. God did not know in advance what human beings would choose. Crescas, on the other hand, maintained that human beings are not free since all their actions are determined by God's foreknowledge. Maimonides held that God has foreknowledge and yet human beings are free. Human foreknowledge, Maimonides asserted, is incompatible with free will but divine foreknowledge is fundamentally different from human knowledge. Therefore divine omniscience is compatible with free will.

A similar debate concerned God's providence. Maimonides and Gersonides defended the doctrine of general providence and linked special providence to enlightened human beings. Only those who are excellent intellectually and morally, they asserted, come under God's special care. Hasidism extended this doctrine further. According to this view, divine providence is over everything since God is the creator of all. Nothing moves without God's causal action.

The problem of evil similarly exercised rabbinic authorities, and here too there were serious differences of opinion. Abraham Ibn Daud maintained that God did not create evil since God is all good. What we conceive as evil, he explained, is actually an absence of good. It is therefore incorrect to say that God created evil. There is in reality no evil; only the absence of good. What could be said instead is that God did not create certain goods for particular people.

Maimonides' view is essentially the same. All evils are privations. Thus God did not create evil but was responsible for the privation of good. In kabbalistic Judaism, evil is seen as positive. According to Lurianic doctrine, God contracted to make room for the world. The light that moved into this great space resulted in the 'breaking of the vessels', and even after the reconstruction of the spheres, some light was poured over to form worlds of decreasing order until eventually it nourished the inhabitants of the evil realm. Evil is thus the result of a cosmic catastrophe.

Another rabbinic controversy concerned the resurrection of the dead. Saadiah Gaon believed that the soul would be reunited with the body and both together would be rewarded or punished. Saadiah believed that both reward and punishment are eternal. Only such limitless reward and punishment, he argued, would provide proper incentives for God's worship, and even eternal punishment is due to God's kindness in the divine desire to make human beings virtuous.

Maimonides' doctrine of the afterlife was essentially spiritual. There would be resurrection of the body, but it would endure for only short time. Ultimately it is the soul that is immortal in the world to come. Maimonides equated hell with the annihilation of the sinner's soul rather than with actual torment. Nahmanides argued that hell is an actual place. It would be unjust, he asserted, to have the same punishment for all the wicked regardless of the severity of their sins.

These rabbinic discussions illustrate that within mainstream Judaism there is great scope for individual interpretation. The theological views of individual teachers are their own opinions, enjoying only as much authority as the teachers' learning. All Jews are obliged to accept the divine origin of the Law, but this is not so with regard to the various theological concepts expounded by the rabbis. For this reason, many modern Jewish thinkers have felt justified in abandoning various elements of traditional rabbinic theology that they no longer regard as tenable.

This flexibility of theological interpretation and doctrine is reflected in the traditional Jewish conversion procedure. The emphasis of Jewish conversion is on joining the community and accepting the Law, not on the convert's personal religious convictions. For this reason converts are told of the persecution and discrimination that Jews have endured through the ages. As members of the Jewish community, they might well suffer similar indignities. Further, converts are made aware of the legal obligations they must assume as Jews. The conversion ceremony is thus regarded as a legal rite of passage by which the converts will take their place within the community.

Summary

We can see, therefore, that the Jewish tradition places halakhic [legal] observance at its centre. Though the Jewish faith is based on belief in God's action in history and revelation of the Torah, individual theological speculation is not regarded as authoritative. The Law, as contained in the Torah and expanded by the rabbis, is the basis of the religious system. Moral praxis, not theology, is at the heart of the faith. Of primary importance is the translation of religious conviction into concrete behaviour in this world. God's truth is to be fulfilled by deeds of lovingkindness. According to Judaism, faith is the total human response to God. True faith is not a simple affirmation of abstract truths as formulated in a creed, but a commitment, an overall attitude, a particular posture to life. Faith in action – ethical praxis – is the truest expression of religious devotion. Such a recognition of Jewish ethical responsibility is more important than ever in the face of the continuing crisis in the Holy Land.

PART II

Solving the 'Unsolvable'

A Jewish Theology of Liberation compels Jews to view the Middle East conflict in moral terms. In the contemporary world where Jews are often comfortable and affluent, the prophetic message of liberation can easily be forgotten. Yet a theology of liberation – with its focus on the desperate situation of those at the bottom of society – can act as a clarion call, awakening the people of Israel to their divinely appointed task. Jewish tradition points to God's Kingdom as the goal and hope of humankind: a world in which all peoples and nations will turn away from injustice. This is not the hope of bliss in a future life, but the building up of the divine kingdom of truth and peace among all peoples.

For nearly 4,000 years the land of Israel has been at the centre of the Jewish faith. Following the destruction of the Temple by the Romans in 70 CE, the promise of a return to Zion sustained them through persecution and suffering. Now that the Jewish nation has re-established itself in Israel after centuries of exile, what of the future? Arguably what is now needed is for Jews world-wide to work together to bring about a Palestinian state for those in exile. The Jewish longing for statehood has been fulfilled; after nearly a century of suffering, Arabs too must have a homeland of their own in the Holy Land.

Chapter 4
The Conflict

At the middle of the nineteenth century, there were approximately 10,000 Jews living peacefully in the Holy Land. With the rise of Zionism at the end of the century, however, the indigenous Arab population came to fear that the country would be overrun by a massive influx of Jewish immigrants. From the 1920s violence erupted between Jews and their neighbours as Zionism began to take hold of Jewish consciousness world-wide.

The Early Struggle

The quest for a Jewish state was set in motion by the events of the nineteenth century. Following the inspiration of early Zionist leaders, the First Zionist Congress met on 29 August 1897 in the Great Hall of the Basel Municipal Casino under the leadership of Theodor Herzl. Subsequently, Herzl cultivated important figures in Turkey, Austria, Germany and Russia to further his plans. In 1902 a British Royal Commission on Alien Immigration was appointed with Lord Rothschild as one of its members. On 7 July 1902 Herzl appeared before the Commission, declaring that further Jewish immigration to Britain should be accepted but that the ultimate solution to the refugee problem was the recognition of the Jews as a people and the finding by them of a legally recognized home.

This appearance brought Herzl into contact with the Colonial Secretary, Joseph Chamberlain, who subsequently suggested to Herzl that a Jewish homeland could be established in Uganda. Fearful of the plight of Russian Jewry, Herzl was prepared to accept the proposal. As a result, Lord Lansdowne, the Foreign Secretary, wrote to Herzl stating that he would be prepared to entertain favorable proposals for the establishment of a Jewish colony of settlement. After Herzl read Lansdowne's letter to the Zionist Congress, a number of Russian delegates who viewed the Uganda Plan as a betrayal of Zionism walked out. At the next Congress, Uganda was formally rejected as a place for a national homeland.

In Britain Chaim Weizmann pressed for the acceptance of the Zionist proposal. In a meeting with the Foreign Secretary, Sir Edward Grey, on 9 November 1914, the Jewish British statesman Herbert Samuel asked about a homeland for the Jewish people. In reply, Grey said that the idea had always had a strong sentimental attachment for him, and he would be prepared to work for it if the opportunity arose. Later in the day, Samuel attempted to enlist the support of Lloyd George, the Chancellor of the Exchequer. When Samuel later put his plan to the Cabinet it was resisted by his cousin Edwin Montague. During this period Weizmann pressed on with his plans.

Later in the year, when Lloyd George became prime minister and Arthur Balfour was appointed Foreign Secretary, the Zionist cause was given a more sympathetic hearing. In January 1917 the Tsar was overthrown and the provisional prime minister, Kerensky, ended Russia's antisemitic code. At the end of the month Germany engaged in U-boat warfare, thereby drawing America on to the Allied side. In the light of these events, the US government became a supporter of a Jewish home in Palestine. In the same year Balfour, as Foreign Secretary, wrote to Lord Rothschild, the head of the English Jewish community, promising British commitment to a Jewish homeland in Palestine. The original draft of this letter (the text of which was agreed on beforehand by both sides) stated that Palestine should be reconstituted as a whole as a Jewish national home with internal autonomy, and that there should be an unrestricted right of Jewish immigration. This document was not approved by the Cabinet until 31 October 1917, but substantial changes were made. Palestine was not equated with the national home, nor was there any reference to unrestricted Jewish immigration. Further, the rights of the Arabs were safeguarded.

The central passage of the letter, subsequently known as the Balfour Declaration, read:

> His Majesty's Government view with favour the establishment in Palestine of a national home for the Jewish people, and will use their best endeavors to facilitate the achievement of this object, it being clearly understood that nothing shall be done which may prejudice the civil and religious rights of existing non-Jewish communities in Palestine, or the rights and political status enjoyed by Jews in any other country.

A month after the Balfour Declaration was published, General Allenby captured Jerusalem. When Weizmann went to meet him in 1918, Allenby was overwhelmed by military and administrative difficulties. Weizmann was told the time was not propitious to implement the British plan: 'Nothing can be done at present,' he stated. 'We have to be extremely careful not to hurt the susceptibilities of the population.' Yet despite such obstacles, as well as opposition from various quarters, Britain secured the Palestinian Mandate at the peace negotiations and steps were taken to create a national Jewish homeland.

With the rise of Arab nationalism, the Jewish settlements in Palestine came increasingly under threat. In March 1920 Arabs attacked Jewish settlements in Galilee when the Russian war hero Joseph Trumpeldor was killed; this was followed by Arab riots in Jerusalem. In response, Vladimir Jabotinsky's self-defence force went into action and Jabotinsky and others were arrested, tried by a military court, and given fifteen years' hard labour. Arab rioters were also convicted and imprisoned. Following these events, Lloyd George sent out Herbert Samuel, as High Commissioner, to the fury of the Arab population. Intent on implementing the Balfour Deceleration – which aimed to safeguard the civil and religious rights of non-Jewish communities – Samuel criticized the Zionists for failing to recognize the importance of Arab nationalist aspirations.

Despite such cautionary advice, the Zionists had few resources for appeasing the Arab population in the early 1920s and were therefore not anxious to heed Samuel's words. Nonetheless, Samuel pursued a policy of even-handedness, pardoning the Arab extremists who had started the riots of 1921. Following this act, he confirmed Sheikh Hisam, who was elected Grand Mufti of Jerusalem by the electoral college of pious Muslims, in preference to the extremist Hajj Amin Al-Husseini. Subsequently the Al-Husseini family and the nationalist wing who had led the 1920 riots embarked on a campaign against the electoral college. Throughout Jerusalem they put up posters which proclaimed: 'The accursed traitors, whom you all know, have combined with the Jews to have one of their party appointed Mufti.'

Within the British staff, an anti-Zionist, Ernst T. Richmond (who acted as an adviser to the High Commissioner on Muslim affairs), persuaded Sheikh Hisam to step down and urged Samuel to allow Hajj Amin to take his place. On 11 July 1921 Samuel saw Hajj Amin, who gave assurances that he and his family would be dedicated to peace. Three weeks later riots occurred in Jaffa and elsewhere in which forty-five Jews were killed. This error of judgment was compounded when Samuel fostered the creation of a supreme Muslim Council which was transformed by the Mufti and his followers into a means of terrorizing the Jewish population. Further, Samuel encouraged Palestinian Arabs to contact their neighbours to promote Pan-Arabism. As a result, the Mufti was able to generate anti-Zionist feeling within the Pan-Arab movement.

Although the British government initially agreed that all Jews should be free to emigrate to Palestine, immigration eventually became a pressing issue. After the Arab riots, Samuel suspended Jewish immigration, and three boatloads of Jews fleeing from Poland and the Ukraine were sent back from Israel. According to Samuel, mass migration could not be allowed. Not surprisingly this policy led to vehement Jewish protests. Under Samuel's successor, Lord Plumer, the country prospered, yet Jewish resentment continued. Although Weizmann adopted a moderate stance towards Palestinian development, other leaders such as Jabotinsky were more impatient. In 1922 Churchill ended the ban on immigration, but his White Paper nonetheless insisted that immigration must reflect the economic capacity of the country. Unwilling to accept British policy, Jabotinsky believed that immigration should be the sole concern of Jewish authorities. On this basis, he left the Zionist executive in 1923 and in 1925 founded the Union of Zionist-Revisionists, which sought to attract the largest number of Jews in the shortest possible time. This movement was hailed in Eastern Europe where its youth wing, Betar, wore uniforms and received military training.

The Creation of Israel

Despite the efforts to encourage Jewish immigration, the Jewish population in Palestine grew only gradually. By 1927 only 2,713 immigrants had arrived whereas 5,000 Jews had left the country. Three years later the number of arrivals and departures was about the same. But from 1929, as the economic and political situation grew worse throughout Europe, a large number of Jews sought to enter the country. In 1929 a massacre took place in Palestine in which 150 Jews were killed. This led to a further limit on immigration despite the fact that hundreds of thousands of Jews sought entry into Palestine. As more and more Jews were allowed to settle, Arab resentment intensified. Each year there were more than 30,000 arrivals, and in 1935 the number grew to 62,000.

In response a major Arab uprising took place in April 1936. On 7 July 1937 a commission headed by Lord Peel recommended that Jewish immigration be reduced to 12,000 a year, and restrictions were placed on land purchases. In addition a three-way partition was suggested. The coastal strip, Galilee and the Jezreel valley were to be formed into a Jewish state, whereas the Judaean hills, the Negev and Ephraim would be the Arab state. This plan was rejected by the Arabs and another revolt took place in 1937. In the following year the Pan-Arab conference in Cairo adopted a policy whereby all Arab communities pledged they would take action to prevent further Zionist expansion.

After the failure of the tripartite plan in London in 1939 the British abandoned the policy of partition. In May 1939 a new White Paper was published stating that only 75,000 more Jews would be admitted over five years, and thereafter none except with Arab agreement. At the same time Palestine should proceed with plans to become independent. Although there were then about 500,000 Jews in Palestine, the Arabs still constituted the majority in the country. As a result, the Arabs would be in a position to seize control of Palestine and expel the Jewish people.

Although the Jews supported the Allies, Jewry was committed to overturning British policy as enshrined in the 1939 White Paper. During this period the British attempted to prevent illegal immigrants from landing in Palestine: if their ships got through they were captured and deported. In November 1940 the *Patria*, which was about to set sail for Mauritius carrying 1,700 deportees, was sabotaged by the Haganah; it sank in Haifa Bay with the loss of 250 refugees. Two years later the *Struma*, a refugee ship from Romania, was refused landing permission, turned back by the Turks and sunk in the Black Sea with the death of 770 passengers.

In 1943, Menahem Begin, formerly chairman of Betar, took over control of the Irgun. With 600 agents under his control he blew up various British buildings. On 6 November 1944 the ultra-extreme group, the Stern Gang, murdered Lord Moyne, the British Minister for Middle Eastern Affairs. Outraged by this act, the Haganah launched a campaign against both the Sternists and the Irgun. While he was fighting the British and other Jews, Begin organized a powerful underground force in the belief that the Haganah would eventually join him in attacking the British. In 1945 a united Jewish Resistance movement was created which embraced the various Jewish military forces, and on 31 October it began blowing up railways. In retaliation, the British made a raid on the Jewish Agency on 29 June 1946. Begin, however, persuaded the Haganah to blow up the King David Hotel where a segment of the British administration was located. When Weizmann heard of this plan he was incensed, and the Haganah was ordered to desist. Begin refused and on 22 July 1946 the explosion took place, killing 27 British, 41 Arabs, 17 Jews and 3 others. The British then proposed a tripartite plan of partition which was rejected by both Jews and Arabs. Exasperated by this conflict, the British Foreign Secretary, Ernest Bevin, declared he was handing over the dispute to the United Nations.

Due to the ongoing conflict, the British resolved that they would leave Palestine as soon as possible. In May 1947 the Palestinian question came before the United Nations, and a special committee was authorized to formulate a plan for the future of the country. The minority recommended a binational state, but the majority suggested that there be both an Arab Jerusalem and a Jewish state as well as an international zone in Jerusalem. On 29 November this recommendation was endorsed by the General Assembly.

After this decision was taken, the Arabs began to attack Jewish settlements. Although the Jewish commanders were determined to repel this assault, their resources were inferior to those on the Arab side. The Haganah had 17,600 rifles, 2,700 sten-guns, about 1,000 machine guns, and approximately 20,000–43,000 men in various stages of training. The Arabs, on the other hand, had a sizable liberation army as well as the regular forces of the Arab states including 10,000 Egyptians, 7,000 Syrians, 3,000 Iraqis, and 3,000 Lebanese as well as 4,500 soldiers from the Arab Legion of Transjordan. By March 1948 over 1,200 Jews had been killed; in April, David Ben-Gurion ordered the Haganah to link the Jewish enclaves and consolidate as much territory as possible under the United Nations plan. Jewish forces then occupied Haifa, opened up the route to Tiberius and eastern Galilee, and captured Safed, Jaffa and Acre. On 14 May David Ben-Gurion read out the Scroll of Independence in the Tel Aviv Museum:

> By virtue of our national and intrinsic right and on the strength of the Resolution of the United Nations General Assembly, we hereby declare the establishment of the Jewish state in Palestine, which shall be known as the State of Israel.

War between Israel and the Arab World

On 11 June a truce was concluded, but in the next month conflict broke out and the Israelis seized Lydda, Ramleh and Nazareth, as well as large areas beyond the partition frontiers. Within ten days the Arabs agreed to another truce, but outbreaks of hostility continued. In mid-October the Israelis attempted to open the road to the Negev settlements and took Beersheba. On 12 January 1949 armistice talks took place in Rhodes and an armistice was later signed by Egypt, Lebanon, Transjordan and Syria. These events created the ongoing Arab–Palestinian problem: 656,000 Arab inhabitants fled from Israeli-held territories: 280,000 to the West Bank; 70,000 to Transjordan; 100,000 to Lebanon; 4,000 to Iraq; 75,000 to Syria; 7,000 to Egypt; and 190,000 to the Gaza Strip.

On the basis of the 1949 armistice, the Israelis sought agreement on the boundaries of the Jewish state. The Arabs, however, refused to consider this proposal – instead they insisted that Israel return to the 1947 partition lines, without giving any formal recognition of the new state. Further, despite the concluding of the armistice, fedayeen bands continued to attack Israeli citizens, and boycotts and blockades sought to injure Israel's economy. After King Abdullah was assassinated on 20 June 1951, a military junta ousted the Egyptian monarch; on 25 February 1954 President Gemal Abdul Nasser gained control of the country. From September 1955 the Soviet bloc supplied weapons to the Arabs, and this encouraged Nasser to take steps against the Jewish State. From 1956 he denied Israeli ships access to the Gulf of Aqaba. In April 1956 he signed a pact with Saudi Arabia and Yemen, and in July he seized the Suez Canal. Fearing Arab intentions, Israel launched a pre-emptive strike on 29 October, and in the war that followed, Israel captured all of Sinai as well as Gaza, and opened a sea route to Aqaba.

At the end of the Sinai War, Israel undertook to withdraw from Sinai as long as Egypt did not remilitarize it, and UN forces formed a protective *cordon sanitaire*. This arrangement endured for ten years, but attacks still continued during this period. In 1967, Nasser launched another offensive and on 15 May he moved 100,000 men and armour into Sinai and expelled the UN army. On 22 May he blockaded Aqaba; several days later King Hussein of Jordan signed a military agreement in Cairo. On the same day, Iraqi forces took up positions in Jordan. In the face of this Arab threat, Israel launched a strike on 5 June, destroying the Egyptian air force on the ground. On 7 June the Israeli army took the Old City, thereby making Jerusalem its capital. On the next day the Israeli forces occupied the entire Left Bank, and in the days the followed captured the Golan Heights and reoccupied Sinai.

Despite such a crushing defeat, the Six-Day War did not bring security to the Jewish State. Nasser's successor, President Anwar Sadat, expelled Egypt's Soviet military advisers in July 1972, cancelled the country's political and military alliance with other Arab states, and together with Syria attacked Israel on Yom Kippur, 6 October 1973. At the outbreak of war, the Egyptians and the Syrians broke through Israeli defences, but by 9 October the Syrian advance had been repelled. On 10 October the American President, Richard Nixon, began an airlift of advanced weapons to Israel; two days later the Israelis engaged in a counterattack on Egypt and moved towards victory. On 24 October a cease-fire came into operation.

After the the Labour coalition lost the May 1977 election and handed over power to the Likud, headed by Menahem Begin, Sadat offered to negotiate peace terms with Israel. On 5 September 1978, at the American presidential home Camp David, the process of reaching such an agreement began and was completed thirteen days later. The treaty specified that Egypt would recognize Israel's right to exist and provide secure guarantees for her southern border. In return Israel would hand over Sinai. In addition she would undertake to negotiate away much of the West Bank and make concessions over Jerusalem as long as a complementary treaty was agreed with the Palestinians and other Arab countries. This latter step, however, was never taken – the proposal was rejected by the Palestinian Arabs. This meant that Israel was left with the responsibility for overseeing Arab occupied territories.

In the years that followed, Arab influence grew immeasurably, due to the Arab's control of oil in the Middle East. As the price of oil increased, Arab revenue provided huge sums for the purchase of armaments. At the UN the Arab world exerted its power, and in 1975 the General Assembly passed a Resolution equating Zionism with racism. Further, Yasser Arafat, the leader of the Palestine Liberation Organization, was accorded head of government status by the UN. Fearing the growing threat of Palestinian influence and terrorism, Israel launched an advance into southern Lebanon in June 1982, destroying PLO bases. This Israeli onslaught and subsequent occupation served as the background to the killing of Muslim refugees by Christian Falangist Arabs in the Sabra and Shatila camps on 16 September 1982. Throughout the world this atrocity was portrayed as Israel's fault. In response to this criticism, the Israeli government ordered an independent judicial inquiry which placed some blame on the Israeli Minister of Defense, Ariel Sharon, for not having prevented this massacre.

The *Intifada*

After the Israeli conquest during the Yom Kippur War, the State of Israel took control of the Occupied Territories. In the following years the Palestinians staged demonstrations, strikes and riots against Israeli rule. By 1987 the Palestinians in the West Bank and Gaza were largely young educated people who had benefited from formal education. Yet despite such educational advances, they suffered from limited job expectations and this situation led to political radicalism. Such frustration came to a head on 9 December 1987 in Jabaliya, the most militant of the Gaza refugee camps. An Israeli patrol was trapped there during a protest about the death of four residents who were killed in a road accident the previous day. The soldiers shot their way out, killing one youth and wounding ten others. This event provoked riots throughout the Occupied Territories. By January 1989 the Israel Defense Forces stated that 352 Palestinians had died, more than 4,300 were wounded and 25,600 arrested. In addition, 200 Arab homes had been sealed or demolished. As hostilities increased, the *Intifada* (resistance) demonstrated that occupying the West Bank and the Gaza Strip would be a perpetual problem.

The Jewish state was unprepared for such a situation, and the army was forced to improvise. As time passed, the *Intifada* became more resilient and its tactics changed to ambushes, small-scale conflicts and selective strikes. In addition, the technology of modern communications (including radio, telefax and photocopying) were used to apply pressure against the Israelis. In the view of many observers, this uprising had transformed the Palestinian people. Despite having such an impact, the *Intifada* created tensions within the Palestinian community. As the resistance developed, Islamic revivalism spread from the Gaza Strip to the West Bank and Jerusalem and posed a serious threat to secular Palestinian nationalism Such a division was aggravated when the PLO endorsed a two-stage solution to the Palestinian problem. Such a policy was bitterly condemned by fundamentalists. Hamas, the Islamic Resistance Movement, insisted on a Muslim Palestine from the Mediterranean to the Jordan. Clause 11 of its Manifesto declared:

> The Islamic Resistance Movement believes that all the land of Palestine is sacred to Islam, through all the generations and forever, and it is forbidden to abandon it or part of it. No Arab state individually has this right, nor do all of the Arab states collectively, nor does any king or president individually, nor do all the kings and presidents collectively. No organization individually has the right, nor do all the organizations collectively, whether they are Palestinian or Arab.

Yasser Arafat, however, adopted a more pragmatic approach and abandoned such maximalist formulations of the Palestinian position in favour of a policy which took into account the reality of Israel's existence.

From the Israeli side, the Israel Defense Forces viewed the *Intifada* in the context of Israel's relationship with its Palestinian neighbours and the world in general. As a result, General Shomron ruled out the use of massive force in dealing with this issue. The *Intifada*, he stated, would end at some point. But the question remained what legacy it would leave. According to General Shomron, the residents of the territories would always be Israel's neighbours. Therefore there would be little point in causing great suffering. Similarly, Brigadier-General Zevi Poleg, who took over as commander of the Israel Defense Forces in the Gaza strip in 1988 stressed that the *Intifada* was not a war. Declaring that he was a military commander, he stressed that it was vital to consider the various aspects of the problem, not just through gunsights but as a human dilemma. If a local person gets hurt, he maintained, you must remember that he is a person, he wasn't born in order for someone to kill him – he was born to live. So, if there is no absolute need to shoot, don't do so.

Despite such a stance, the *Intifada* was generally regarded as more than a local skirmish, and throughout the world Israelis were viewed as guilty of brutality. As a result, there was a growing feeling that Israel should abandon the Occupied Territories. Thus a poll conducted by Professor Elihu Katz, Director of the Hebrew University's Israel Institute of Applied Social Research, in January

1989 revealed considerable sympathy towards the idea of a Palestinian state. Concluding his findings, he wrote:

> Some 30 per cent of Israeli Jews (half of the Left and 10–20 per
> cent of the Right) are willing to grant essential prerequisites for
> a Palestinian state: Negotiations, substantial territorial conces-
> sions and recognition. If questions are worded to make evident
> that security and peace might be obtained in exchange for these
> concessions, the favorable proportion increases substantially to
> 30 per cent or more.
>
> (Silver, 'The Intifada and After', *Survey of Jewish Affairs*,
> p. 12)

Thus after several years of Palestinian revolt in the Occupied Territories, the Israeli population appeared more prepared to settle its
dispute with its Arab inhabitants, as has been evidenced by subsequent peace talks between Israel and the Palestinians.

The Road to Peace

In December 1991 a conference took place in Washington dealing with procedures for future talks between the Israelis and the
Palestinians. Israel insisted it was not willing to discuss territorial
concessions; rather it desired to focus on Palestinian autonomy.
The Palestinians, however, were not content with such a limitation. After these talks, Jews and Arabs met in a number of cities to
explore various practical issues. The first of these talks took place in
Moscow and focused on water sharing and economic co-operation.
In Ottawa the refugee problem was of central importance, whereas
in Vienna water sharing was of critical significance. In Brussels the
main topic was economic co-operation.

Such collaborative ventures were interrupted by the Israeli
election in June, in which Labour became the largest party, form-
ing an alliance with the left-wing party Meretz and the Arab Democratic Party. Shas, too, joined the coalition. As prime minister,
Yitzhak Rabin was committed to continuing the peace process as
well as the absorption of Russian immigrants into the country. On
19 July, James Baker arrived in the Middle East to seek a solution
to the conflict between Israel and its neighbours. As these efforts

continued, tension mounted in the West Bank and Jerusalem during November and December 1993. The efforts to renew the peace process inflamed members of Hamas and Islamic Jihad, who were bitterly opposed to compromise. With the encouragement of Iran, Hamas condemned the Israeli occupation while improving its educational, welfare and health care of the Palestinian population.

In January, at a villa outside Oslo, representatives met for three days. At the meeting several of the PLO submitted proposals involving the Israeli withdrawal from the Gaza Strip, a mini Marshall Plan for the West Bank and Gaza, and economic co-operation between Israel and the Palestinian authorities. At the beginning of February the Oslo talks continued, and a draft declaration of principles was drawn up, as well as a paper establishing guidelines for a regional Marshall Plan. Between 20 and 22 March secret meetings took place in Oslo, in which it seemed that an accord between Israel and the PLO might emerge. This was followed by another meeting on 14 June; two months later the Oslo Accords were approved by both the Israelis and the Palestinians. After the PLO had been required to renounce terrorism, a ceremony took place in Washington on 13 September 1993 with Yitzhak Rabin and Yasser Arafat as the main representatives. In the following months Israel and the PLO engaged in active negotiations for an Israeli withdrawal from the West Bank and the Gaza Strip.

These developments were interrupted on 25 February when an Israeli gunman opened fire on Palestinian Arabs inside the main mosque in Hebron. In response to this massacre, Arafat broke off his negotiations with Israel, yet after several weeks of pressure the talks were resumed. On 3 May Rabin and Arafat met in Cairo to finalize a peace agreement. Despite further disturbances, the peace process continued, and a meeting of 2,500 Israeli, Arab, American and European politicians and business people met in Casablanca for an economic summit which was addressed by Peres and Rabin. On 29 March 1995 British Prime Minister John Major arrived in Israel for a meeting with Rabin. Among the Palestinians, there was bitter conflict between those who supported efforts to achieve autonomy and those who rejected any form of negotiation with Israel.

Determined to continue the peace process, Peres went to Gaza on 4 July for a meeting with Arafat to finalize Oslo II, the extension of

Palestinian rule to the West Bank accompanied by the withdrawal of Israeli troops. Under this scheme the West Bank would eventually be ruled by Palestinian authorities. On 22 September Peres and Arafat went to an Egyptian resort and discussed the final aspects of Palestinian rule in the West Bank. The next week Rabin flew to Washington, where he signed the Oslo II agreement. The opposition parties denounced Rabin, calling him a traitor to his country. At a rally in Jerusalem on 28 October, Rabin was shot and killed by a fervent Jew. This event profoundly disrupted the peace process, and the Oslo agreement came under increasing pressure.

In October 1998 Prime Minister Netanyahu and Yasser Arafat met in Washington. After prolonged argument, Israel and the Palestinians agreed to embark on a new stage of co-operation. According to the Wye Agreement, Israel would effect a further West Bank redeployment, involving 27.2 per cent of the occupied territory. Arafat agreed that the Palestinian authorities would take all necessary measures to prevent acts of terrorism, crime and hostilities. This would include a Palestinian security plan, shared with the United States to ensure a systematic and effective combat of terrorist organizations and infrastructure. To ensure peace in the region, bilateral Israeli–Palestinian security co-ordination would be restored, and a US–Palestinian committee would be created to monitor militant groups. The Palestinians further agreed to apprehend, investigate and prosecute specific individuals suspected of violence. It was accepted they would collect all illegally held weapons in areas they controlled, and issue a decree barring any form of incitement to violence or terror. To ensure the implementation of this policy, a US–Palestinian–Israeli committee would monitor any cases of incitement.

In the midst of these negotiations Ariel Sharon angered Palestinians by visiting the Temple Mount in Jerusalem. Dozens of police and several Palestinians were injured in the riots that followed. On 4 October, Prime Minister Ehud Barak and Yasser Arafat flew to France to meet the US Secretary of State Madeleine Albright and French President Jacques Chirac. Despite such political activity, fighting between the two sides continued. By July 2000 negotiations for a final settlement resulted in a deadlock: Palestinians insisted that refugees should have the right to return to their former homeland – this would have led to a Palestinian majority in the country. Israel insisted on annexing key portions of the Palestinian areas, leaving most settlements intact, and offered only a limited form of Palestinian statehood. Nonetheless, in January 2001 peace talks were held in at Taba, an Egyptian town.

At this meeting Israeli and Palestinian representatives agreed that in accordance with UN Security Council Resolution 242, the 4 June 1967 lines would form the basis for borders between Israel and the State of Palestine. For the first time both sides presented their own maps regarding the West Bank. The Israelis stated they did not need to maintain settlements in the Jordan Valley for security purposes, and both sides accepted the principle of land exchange and sovereignty for their respective areas. Concerning the future of Jerusalem, both sides accepted in principle the suggestion that the Palestinians should have sovereignty over Arab neighbourhoods and Israel should have sovereignty over Jewish sections. The Israelis agreed that Jerusalem should become the capital of both states. Further, both parties accepted the principle of respective control over each side's holy sites. The refugee problem was to be resolved in accordance with UN Security Council Resolution 242 and General Assembly Resolution 194. Finally, the Israeli side maintained that the State of Palestine would be non-militarized; the Palestinian side was prepared to accept limitation on its acquisition of arms.

Renewed Conflict

Following these discussions at Taba, an Israeli election took place and Ehud Barak was voted out of office and replaced by a right-wing government headed by Ariel Sharon. Following this victory, Sharon rejected Palestinian demands to resume peace talks where they had left off with the outgoing administration of Ehud Barak. In April 2001 the Mitchell report was published, which made a series of wide-ranging recommendations. The report concluded that it was vital that the government of Israel and the Palestinian Authority (PA) act swiftly and decisively to halt violence. The immediate objective of the report was to rebuild confidence and resume negotiations. Despite attempts by the Mitchell commission and others to restore peace, violence continued on both sides. On 11 September 2001, Al-Qaeda terrorists hijacked airliners and flew them into the World Trade Center in New York and the Pentagon outside Washington.

Following the attack on the twin towers of the World Trade Center and the offensive against Bin Laden, Arab and Islamic countries stressed the need for their co-operation in the war against terrorism in order to obtain concessions from Israel. However, many Americans began to lose sympathy for the Palestinian cause, identifying Hamas and Hezbollah with the Al-Qaeda group of terrorists. Palestinians were criticized for their apparent support of Bin Laden. On 12 March 2002 the UN Security Council passed Resolution 1397, a US-drafted resolution, referring for the first time to a Palestinian state existing side by side with Israel. In retaliation for Palestinian attacks on Israelis, Israel launched a massive raid intended to root out the Palestinian terror network including reoccupation of Ramallah, Nablus, Jenin, Tulkarm and other towns. The Israeli onslaught, referred to as Operation Defensive Shield, commenced on 28 March 2002. Its goal was to dismantle the terrorist infrastructure developed by the Palestinian Authority, or allowed to operate in territory under PA control. The operation consisted of moving Israeli forces into the West Bank and Gaza for the purpose of arresting terrorists, finding and confiscating weapons and destroying facilities for the manufacture of explosives. In March 2003 the Palestine–Israeli conflict was eclipsed by the American and British attack on Iraq, overthrowing the regime of Sadam Hussein. Prior to this conflict President George W. Bush reiterated his desire for a solution to the Palestinian problem in the Middle East, yet in the Arab world the onslaught against Iraq was widely perceived as a Crusade against Islam.

During this period the United States expressed its refusal to negotiate with Yasser Arafat, and Mahmoud Abbas began to emerge as a more acceptable figure. Abbas's term as prime minister was characterized by various conflicts between him and Arafat regarding the distribution of power. In addition, he came into conflict with Palestinian militant groups including Islamic Jihad and Hamas over his moderate policies. In May 2004 Israel launched Operation Rainbow in the Gaza Strip; several months later Operation Days of Penitence began. In November 2004 Yasser Arafat died, and Mahmoud Abbas was elected president in January 2005. During this period, the Israeli unilateral disengagement plan was adopted by the government – its aim was to remove the permanent Israeli presence in the Gaza Strip as well as four settlements in the northern West Bank. Civilians were evacuated and residential buildings demolished.

In January 2006 Fatah and Hamas candidates competed for seats in the Palestinian Legislative Council. Due to widespread dissatisfaction with Fatah, Hamas won a majority of seats and was thereby able to appoint a prime minister as well as a number of cabinet posts. Alarmed by these developments, the West branded Hamas a terrorist organization and cut off aid to the Palestinian government in March 2006, insisting it recognize Israel, renounce violence and accept the peace process. Israel refused to negotiate with Hamas since it has never abandoned its conviction that Israel has no right to exist and that the entire State of Israel is an illegal occupation. On 14 April 2006 Ehud Olmert was elected prime minister of Israel. In June 2006 a war commenced between Israel and Hezbollah when Hezbollah fighters entered Israel, attacked an Israel Defense Force post and captured several soldiers. In response Israel attacked Hezbollah positions within Lebanon.

During this period of instability, international sanctions against Hamas and the PA resulted in economic and political difficulties for the Palestinian people. During November 2006 there were efforts by Abbas to form a unity government with Hamas, but this produced no tangible results. In January 2007, fighting continued between Hamas and Fatah. In February President Abbas and Prime Minister Haniyeh met in Saudi Arabia to discuss the Palestinian conflict. It was agreed that Hamas would dissolve the existing government and form a unity coalition with Fatah. During this period diplomatic efforts were initiated to bring about a peaceful solution to the Middle East conflict. In early 2007, Amir Peretz and Efraim Sneh of Israel's Labour party announced their own multi-stage plan for a new peace process – this evoked considerable debate, but their plan lacked credibility. In January 2007, US Secretary of State Condoleezza Rice announced on a visit to Egypt that the US would organize a summit between Israel and the Palestinians. In February 2007 a meeting was held in Israel which included Secretary Rice, Prime Minister Olmert and President Abbas. The next month Japan proposed a peace plan based on common economic development.

In late April 2007 the armed wing of Hamas declared that the truce with Israel had ended; Palestinian groups then launched rockets from the Gaza Strip into Israel. On 25 April 2007 Ehud Olmert ruled out a major Gaza offensive, but authorized the army to carry out limited operations in the Gaza Strip. This led to a new round of Hamas rocket attacks. Israel then stated that it would not carry out a major offensive in order for a new truce to begin.

In May 2007 a deal between Hamas and Fatah appeared to be fading and new fighting broke out. In response to rocket fire from the Gaza Strip, Israel launched air strikes against various targets. In June 2007 full-scale fighting broke out between factions in several communities, and Hamas won control of the entire Gaza Strip, establishing a separate Gaza Strip government. In response, Israel, the US and other Western countries sought to strengthen Fatah and thereby isolate Hamas. Although Fatah was defeated in Gaza, it retained control of the West Bank. In the ensuing months steps were taken to resume the peace process. In November 2007 Israeli and Palestinian leaders agreed to restart peace talks at a Maryland summit, promising further negotiations towards a peace treaty and the development of a Palestinian state. A fragile sixth-month truce between Hamas and Israel expired on 19 December 2008, and was followed by a fierce Israeli bombardment of the Gaza Strip which targeted Hamas bases, police training camps, police headquarters and offices. Hamas intensified its rocket and mortar attacks against targets in Israel throughout this conflict. On 3 January 2009 an Israeli ground invasion began which resulted in the deaths of more than 1,300 Palestinians.

Since 2009 the Obama administration has repeatedly pressured the Israeli government led by Prime Minister Benjamin Netanyahu to freeze the growth of Israeli settlements in the West Bank and reignite the peace process. On 25 November 2009, Israel imposed a ten-month construction freeze on all of its settlements in the West Bank. Eventually, on 2 September 2010, the United States launched direct negotiations between Israel and the Palestinians in Washington. Nevertheless, soon afterwards, when Israel's partial moratorium on settlement construction in the West Bank was about to expire, the Palestinian leadership announced that they planned to leave the negotiations if the moratorium was not renewed. During

September 2011 the Palestinian Authority led a diplomatic campaign aimed at getting UN recognition of the State of Palestine within the 1967 borders with East Jerusalem as its capital. The next month a deal was reached between Israel and Hamas, by which the kidnapped Israeli soldier Gilad Shalit was to be released in exchange for over a thousand Palestinians and Arab-Israeli prisoners.

Summary

As the Zionist movement gathered strength in the first few decades of the nineteenth century, the Arab population of Palestine became increasingly alarmed. Aware of the Zionist quest to create a sizable Jewsh homeland in the Holy Land, violence broke out between Arabs and these early Jewish settlers. From the outset, the native residents of Palestine were determined to protect their country from foreign immigration. The Balfour Declaration of 1917 was regarded as the imposition of colonial aspirations and firmly rejected. When the United Nations agreed to partition Palestine in 1947, the Arabs were unprepared to make any concessions, and war broke out immediately after David Ben-Gurion proclaimed Israel's Declaration of Independence on 14 May 1948. This conflict was followed by a series of wars between Israel and its neighbours. In recent years, numerous attempts have made to solve the Middle East conflict, yet to date there has been no successful solution.

Chapter 5

The Palestinian Argument

The Ottoman Empire, of which Palestine was a part at the time of the Balfour Declaration, had over the centuries provided a refuge for Jews fleeing from persecution. Yet Palestinians argue that this did not justify the Zionist programme of massive immigration. In their view, the waves of Jewish settlers who came to live in Palestine in the first few decades of the nineteenth century were colonialists who had usurped their country.

The Zionist Threat

Throughout the nineteenth century there was small-scale Jewish immigration into Palestine. The Ottomans did nothing at this point to prevent immigration; in fact indirectly they contributed to it by issuing laws that encouraged investment. A law of 1867 provided foreigners the right to own lands in the Ottoman Empire. This resulted in helping Zionists to acquire land in Palestine. Yet as this process became more systematic, the first reaction to Jewish immigration occurred towards the end of the century. At this time, representatives of some of the most prominent families in Jerusalem sent a letter to Constantinople expressing their concern about the influx of Jewish immigrants. Initially, Theodor

Herzl, acting on behalf of the Zionists, sought to persuade the Sultan to view the Zionist plan favourably; at one point he asked for the area from Haifa and Akka to the Transjordan and the Dead Sea to serve as a Jewish refuge. The Sultan refused this request, and in 1900 issued a proclamation prohibiting the permanent settlement of Jews in the Holy Land.

Until the outbreak of the First World War the British had sought to control whatever parts it could of the Ottoman Empire. Initially, there had been an attempt by Sherif Hussein of Makka to persuade the British High Commissioner in Egypt to grant political and military support, or at least to discover what the British position would be if the Arabs started to rebel against Turkish rule in the Arabian Peninsula. The British did not provide a satisfactory response and indicated they were reluctant to become involved. However, when Turkey declared its support for Germany against Britain and France, the British sought to support the Arabs or any group working against Turkey. A number of secret negotiations were conducted during this period between Sherif Hussein and Sir Henry McMahon, the British High Commissioner in Egypt.

When the Arabs were eventually freed from Turkish domination, they believed they were on the point of self-determination. Yet, such expectations were thwarted by the secret Sykes – Picot agreement between the British and the French, which shared out the entire region between the victors. Such disappointment was intensified by the Balfour Declaration, which was issued before the end of the war. As we have noted, this official document committed the British government to assisting the Jews to acquire a homeland in Palestine. The Arabs were incensed. Uncertain of the outcome of the war, the British government had made a number of conflicting undertakings in order to keep all potentially friendly elements on the side of the Allies.

Although the Balfour Declaration stated that the interests of the indigenous population should not be prejudiced by the creation of a Jewish homeland, the Arabs maintained such actions were fundamentally unjust. The Balfour Declaration was subsequently incorporated into the British Mandate and was given substance in a White Paper (the Churchill Memorandum). In Arab eyes, this was a betrayal of the fundamental rights of the indigenous population.

On what basis, they asked, did the British believe they were entitled to promise to the Zionists a land that belonged to others? By the end of the First World War, the Arabs were incensed that there would be no Arab kingdom in the Middle East. Rather, the entire area was to be divided between the Great Powers.

The first Palestinian conference was convened early in 1919 in Jerusalem. The primary focus of the conference was the question of Zionism and the political future of Palestine. The conference expressed the wish that there should be a unified and fully independent Palestine. Later, a Commission was appointed to spend six weeks in Palestine and Syria. The commission interviewed a large number of delegates from forty towns and rural areas, and received more than 1,800 petitions. Those opposed to the Zionist movement claimed that there was a Zionist plan to displace the indigenous Palestinian population by land purchase and military mobilization in order to enforce mass Jewish immigration. The commission echoed this view, stressing that such a plan would be contrary to the wishes of 90 per cent of the existing population. Such an act, they believed, would violate the principles of self-determination.

The final report, however, did not produce any positive recommendations favourable to the Palestinians. Such disappointment was the background to the civil unrest that took place in Jerusalem in the spring of 1920 during the annual Palestinian festival of al-Nabi Musa. This consisted of demonstrations against both British and Jewish immigration. The same year a further conference was held in Haifa, headed by Musa Karem al-Husseini. At this gathering an executive committee was elected to monitor the situation. The Palestinian leadership attempted to persuade Churchill to change British policy.

At this stage the British Mandatory authority appointed a commission of investigation (the Haycroft Commission) which concluded that the aim of the Zionist movement in Palestine was permanent settlement. During the same year, the Palestinians held their fourth conference in Jerusalem, attended by delegates from throughout the country, which resolved to send a delegation to Europe to explain the Palestinian situation. The High Commissioner, Herbert Samuel, permitted this delegation to travel as individuals but refused to allow them to travel with the status of a body representing the Palestinian people. Initially they met with the Pope; this was followed by trips to Britain and Geneva. Returning to the UK, they published a pamphlet: 'The Holy Land: The Muslim and Christian Case against the Zionist Aggression'. Pressure was applied on the Colonial Office to change its pro-Zionist stance. Urged by the Colonial Office, the Palestinian delegation met with Zionist leaders in the Middle East section of the Colonial Office, but no agreement was reached. Although the British government was willing to modify the terms of the Mandate, it was not prepared to abandon the policy of the Balfour Declaration. Negotiations between the Palestinians and the British continued, but no agreement was reached. The delegation returned to Palestine having failed in its mission.

The White Paper and Beyond

The Churchill White Paper was issued by the British government in 1922; this was originally drafted as a memorandum entitled 'British Policy in Palestine'. On 3 June the draft was communicated to the Zionist Organization. This included a paragraph that put on record the British government's denial of the claim by the Palestinian delegation that Palestine west of the Jordan river was included in the pledge made to Sherif Hussein by Sir Henry McMahon. Among the main principles of the White Paper was the assertion that a Jewish national home would be created in Palestine: the Jewish people would be granted residence in the Holy Land by right, not on sufferance. At the same time, the British were determined that there should be no subordination of the Arab population, language or culture. It was also asserted that Jewish immigration would not exceed the economic capacity of the country.

Once the Mandate was approved, the British government accepted its responsibility to implement the White Paper. Initially the High Commissioner, Sir Herbert Samuel, sought to create a legislative council. However, on their return from London the Palestinian delegates held their fifth conference in Nablus and rejected Samuel's proposal. In response, Samuel abandoned the notion of a legislative council, replacing it with a representative council consisting of eight Muslims, two Christians and two Jews. Meanwhile, the Arabs continued their boycott, believing that such resistance

would be successful. As a further attempt to gain Arab co-operation, the British proposed that an Arab agency be created to administer social affairs for the non-Jewish population; it was also recommended that such a body be consulted regarding immigration.
Such a plan was rejected by the Arab Executive, and the Colonial
Office instructed the High Commissioner to terminate negotiations
with the Arabs and administer the country with an advisory council
consisting of British officials.

In October 1922 the Palestinians sent a delegation to Lausanne
to attend the conference convened to modify the terms of the Treaty
of Sevres. En route the delegation visited Turkey, seeking to gain
Turkish support for the modification of Article 95 which endorsed
the Balfour Declaration. The Turks, however, rejected the Palestinian proposal on the grounds that the loss of their Arab territories was a major factor in the collapse of the Ottoman Empire and
the Turkish defeat in the First World War. In June 1923 the Sixth
Palestinian Arab Congress was held in Jaffa – one of its central
goals was to reform the national movement. During the conference
Sherif Hussein wrote to the Chairman, stating that he had concluded a treaty with the British government which granted British
recognition of Arab independence throughout the Arabian Peninsula except for Aden. The British, however, denied the claim but
asserted that they had no intention of taking steps that would affect
the civil and religious rights of the Arab population. The Congress
decided to reject the treaty, boycott any loans entered into in the
name of Palestine, and to exclude from the Palestinian Executive
any person who accepted the terms of the treaty.

The Congress elected a delegation to travel to London to observe
the negotiations between Sherif Hussein's representative and the
Foreign Office. These negotiations failed because Palestine was not
included in the treaty. There were two options: one was to include
Palestine in the treaty on the basis that the Sherif would accept the
Balfour Declaration and the British would issue an interpretation
stating that it was not intended to lead to the creation of a Jewish
state. The alternative was that Palestine would be taken out of the
equation since there would be unity between Iraq, Transjordan and
the Hejaz. The discussions were severed by the abdication of the
Sherif in favour of his son Ali.

During the period from the issue of the White Paper until 1929 there were no impediments to Jewish immigration into the country. Samuel himself was viewed favorably by the Zionists. At the Seventh Palestinian Arab Congress, which was held in Jerusalem on 20–27 June 1928, a new Executive Committee was created and met on a regular basis. In the same year, civil unrest took place at the Wailing Wall, where Jews came to pray. During the previous year a screen for the segregation of women had been installed on the pavement beside the wall. The Palestinians voiced their objection to the British, who ordered that the screen be removed. As a result, local and international Jewish lobbies expressed their indignation. The British government agreed that only such fixtures as had been permitted under Ottoman rule should be allowed, but this was regarded as unsatisfactory by the Palestinians since the Ottomans had not been concerned with this issue. In August 1929 violence erupted and spread throughout Palestine.

The British sent a commission to investigate; on March 1930 the report appeared, concluding that the outbreak in Jerusalem was from the beginning an Arab attack on Jews. These attacks were vicious and caused wanton destruction of Jewish property. In some cases Jews assaulted Arabs and destroyed property, but these attacks were in most cases retaliation for wrongs committed by Arabs. During this period the General Muslim Conference took place in Jerusalem on 1 November 1929 under the leadership of Hajj Amin al-Husseini. It demanded that the integrity of Muslim holy sites should be protected from any infringement. Simultaneously, the Supreme Muslim Council, over which Hajj Amin presided, began a development in the vicinity of the Wailing Wall.

From 1932 the Palestinian population underwent a crisis. The nationalist movement was failing; the Executive Committee was weak and its decision-making ineffective, and an Islamic Congress was having little impact. The Palestinians had little hope of curtailing Jewish immigration. Such a situation led to popular unrest in 1936, triggered by an attack by three Palestinian Arabs on a Jewish colony near Nablus. The next day, two Palestinians were killed in reprisal. This was followed by civil disturbances, resulting in a 24-hour curfew in Jaffa and Tel Aviv. The next day there was a general strike in Jaffa. The first political support for the uprising in Jaffa came from Nablus. There was a public meeting where it was agreed that Nablus should take a lead in the general struggle. The consensus was that the British were responsible for mass Zionist immigration rather than the Zionists themselves. It was further agreed that the struggle should continue until Palestinian demands were met and that there should be no co-operation with commissions and inquiries. Further, no delegations should be sent to London. The main aim was to curtail Jewish immigration, which was perceived as endangering the livelihood of the local population.

In 1936 a Royal Commission under Lord Peel arrived in Palestine and held public and private sessions. The Palestinians initially boycotted the Royal Commission but later co-operated with the inquiry. The Jewish Agency alleged that Jews and Arabs could live harmoniously. In this light, they accepted the Churchill White Paper, which supported the Balfour Declaration and which sought to protect the interests, language, religion and culture of the Arabs. The Arabs disagreed, strongly denouncing the Jewish national home. Their objections focused on the issue of loss of land, lack of development in the countryside, increased cost of living, loss of jobs, and discrimination against Arabs in employment. What the Arabs demanded was a withdrawal of the Jewish National Home policy and the creation of an Arab state which they believed was in accordance with original British promises.

The Royal Commission concluded that recent disturbances in Palestine were due to two main factors: the desire for Arab independence and the fear of the establishment of a Jewish national home. The report maintained that the Jewish national home had become a reality, and in response to the Arab position it was alleged that the condition of the Arab population had improved under British administration. One of the recommendations of the report was that Palestine be partitioned, as it appeared impossible to satisfy both Jewish and Arab demands. Given that it would not be reasonable to hand over 400,000 Jews to Arab rule, nor for the Jews to become a majority and have authority over one million Palestinian Arabs, Palestine should be divided into independent Jewish and Palestinian areas.

Alarmed by such proposals, the Palestinians refused the partition plan and sent delegations to all Arab countries to express their concern. An Arab Summit, which took place at Bludaan in Syria, issued five main resolutions:

(1) Palestine is an integral and indivisible part of the Arab world.
(2) Partition should be opposed.
(3) The Mandate and the Balfour Declaration should be voided and a treaty should be concluded with the British granting Palestinians independence and sovereignty over Palestine.
(4) Jewish immigration should be restricted.
(5) The relationship between the British and the Arab peoples is conditional upon fulfilling these conditions.

Following this summit, Palestinian leaders intensified their negotiations with Arab regimes to rally support. In 1937 Hajj Amin al-Husseini made official visits to Syria and Saudi Arabia. Yet during this period the British attempted to root out ringleaders of the Palestinian resistance movement by detention and deportation. Hajj Amin was removed from his post and at one point took refuge in the Aqsa mosque and later attempted to escape to Syria but was captured by the Lebanese coastguard, taken to the French High Commissioner, and spent the next two years under house arrest in Lebanon.

The Creation of Israel

As it became obvious that war between Britain and Germany was inevitable, the Palestinians entered into talks with Germany. Aware of this danger, the British began to make concessions to the Palestinians. At a conference in London on 7 February 1939, with both Arab and Jewish delegations, the Arabs demanded that Palestine become independent, the Mandate abolished, and the concept of a Jewish national home be abandoned. The new British policy was enshrined in the 1939 White Paper which reiterated the obligations of the Mandate to secure the creation of a Jewish national home, to safeguard the religious and civil rights of all Palestine's inhabitants, and to place the country under workable political, administrative and economic conditions. The White Paper went on to explain that it was not part of British policy to turn Palestine into a Jewish state and proposed that Jewish immigration should be limited for a period of five years, after which it should be curtailed. It also stated that the High Commissioner would be given powers to prohibit further land transfers.

British policy was vehemently rejected by both Jews and Arabs, and a number of Palestinian leaders began to explore the possibility of opening relations with Germany. They came to the conclusion, however, that Germany could not be relied on to support Palestinian aspirations. In Palestine, scattered armed resistance took place against both the British and the Zionists. Throughout the Second World War, Jewish agencies sought to persuade the British to allow the formation of a Jewish brigade to fight the Nazis. As we have noted, in September 1944 this was agreed and a Jewish brigade was on duty in Italy from March 1945, attached to the British Eighth Army.

As the war progressed, there was increasing unity in the Arab world. On 22 March 1945 the League of Arab States was proclaimed in Cairo and issued a declaration of intent. Regarding Palestine, it was stressed that the Holy Land was an integral part of the Arab world; approval was given to the British undertaking to curtail Jewish immigration, and the conference expressed support for the Arabs of Palestine. The conference insisted that there would be no greater injustice than to solve the Jewish problem in Europe by perpetrating another injustice against the Arabs of Palestine. The following spring the Charter of the League of Arab States was issued, which gave the Council the authority to nominate Palestinian representatives in the League since Palestine was not a full member. The League's policy regarding Palestine was to continue applying pressure on Britain to restrict immigration and land purchase, boycott Jewish products, create a development fund to save Palestinian lands, and create representative offices in capitals throughout the world.

As momentum gathered force for the partition of Palestine, Arab fears intensified. The Arab states represented at the Arab League rejected the recommendations made by the United Nations Special Committee on Palestine, and a decision was made that all borders with Palestine should be reinforced in case of war, and a million pounds was granted as aid to Palestinian defences. Once the UN General Assembly agreed to the plan for partition in

November 1947, the Arabs were outraged. In their view, such a decision to create a foreign state in the middle of the Arab world and place key economic areas under Jewish control was grossly unjust. In their view, partition would give prime agricultural land to the Jews, leaving Palestinians with less hospitable desert areas, stony lands and barren hills. Throughout the Arab world there were popular demonstrations, yet political action was not forthcoming.

On 9 April 1948 the Irgun carried out a massacre of men, women and children in the village of Deir Yassin. The intention of this action was to cause mass panic in surrounding areas, and entire villages fled in fear. These were the final acts of violence which led to the British decision to withdraw from the Mandate and remove their forces from Palestine. On the day following the final with-drawal on 14 May 1948, David Ben-Gurion read out Israel's dec-laration of independence in Tel Aviv. The United States was the first to recognize the newly declared state; this was followed by the Soviet Union. Arab forces, however, entered Palestine. They were made up of 6,000 Jordanians, 9,000 Iraqis, 5,000 Egyptians, 1,000 Syrians, 3,000 Saudis, and about 3,000 volunteers from other Arab countries. On the borders there were a further 4,000 Jordanians, 1,000 Iraqis, 8,000 Egyptians, 1,500 Syrians, 1,800 Lebanese and 3,500 volunteers from other Arab lands.

Following intense conflict, a ceasefire took place and the Political Committee of the Arab League met in Cairo to discuss the situation. On 27 July, Count Folke Bernadotte, the UN special envoy, put forward proposals for an Arab and a Jewish state. The Arab sec-tor would include Transjordan, Jerusalem and part of the Negev; western Galilee and most of the existing Jewish areas were to be included in the Israeli state, and there was to be an independent Jewish municipality in Jerusalem. The port of Haifa and the air-port at Lydda were to be a free zone. The issue of immigration was to be left to the individual states. Both the Jews and the Arab League refused to accept this proposal, and the Arabs presented an alternative plan involving the formation of an interim Palestin-ian government. A series of proposals were to form the basis of a constitution:

(1) Palestine is a united sovereign state.
(2) The Palestinian government was to be a democracy responsible to a legislative council.
(3) There should be security for religious areas and minorities and freedom of worship.
(4) There should be respect for basic freedoms without prejudice on the basis of religion, national or ethnic origin or language.
(5) All religious minorities would be entitled to form organizations which would be subject to the authority of the government.
(6) The constitution would recognize the Hebrew language in Jewish areas.
(7) Any person seeking naturalization would have to be a legal resident and have lived in the country for a period specified by the government.

This proposal was not implemented, and Bernadette asked the Security Council to put pressure on the Arabs to extend the cease-fire. The Arabs refused and conflict resumed on 9 July. Eventually an armistice agreement was reached between Israel and Egypt, followed by later armistice agreements. Faced with the problem of Palestinian refugees, Arab and Israeli delegates met in Lausanne to explore various possibilities. Arab representatives argued that the return of refugees could serve as a basis for establishing peace in the area. The Israeli delegates disagreed. By this stage there were nearly a million Palestinian refugees living in neighbouring countries.

Continuing Conflict

Despite the armistice agreements between Israel and it neighbours, attacks against the Jewish state continued, including the conflict over Suez in 1956. In 1958, Fatah was founded by Yasser Arafat and bases were established in most Arab countries. The same year Nasser summoned Arab leaders to a summit in Cairo to discuss Israel's action to divert water from the River Jordan to the Negev desert. The central concern was that this was being done to strengthen Israel's capacity to absorb large numbers of immigrants. At this meeting Arab representatives delegated a Palestinian leader, Ahmed al-Shukairy, to explore ways to create a representative body of all Palestinians: this ultimately became the Palestine Liberation Organization. Later, an assembly of Palestinians from throughout the world met at an assembly in Jerusalem.

At this time the leadership of Fatah wanted to exhibit its strength. One group proposed launching attacks on Israeli targets. Egypt wanted restraint, but Syria encouraged the idea of immediate assault and opened training camps. Later, Fatah launched several operations, but they were not effective. By the end of October 1966 Syria had given full support to Fatah, but Egypt was not involved. On 4 November, however, Egypt signed a new defence alliance with Syria, thereby committing itself to the liberation of Palestine. By early 1967 both Egypt and Israel were accusing one another of troop build-up on the Syrian front. As we noted previously, the Six-Day War began on 5 June 1967, ending with a massive Arab defeat. Israel thereby became the dominant power in the Middle East. Israeli troops were stationed in the Suez Canal, the Red Sea and the River Jordan and held a line on Syria only thirty miles from Damascus. They controlled the whole of the country, including the banks of the Jordan and Jerusalem, along with one million Palestinians in the West Bank and Gaza Strip. Further, they occupied the Sinai Peninsula and a thousand square miles of Syrian territory on the Golan Heights. Approximately one million Arabs had been displaced. Some 350,000 Palestinians fled from the West Bank to the East Bank of the Jordan. For at least 150,000 Palestinians, this was the second time they had been made refugees. A further 160,000 people were refugees in Syria from the villages and farms of the Golan Heights.

Following Israel's victory, Egypt continued to launch a campaign of attacks, aimed at bolstering Arab morale and at the same time disrupting Israeli life. At a Fatah meeting in Damascus after the war, Palestinians representatives discussed what their next step should be. Yasser Arafat was convinced the struggle should continue. Trips were made to the West Bank to encourage fellow Palestinians. Yet Fatah's attempt to create an armed revolution in the West Bank was ineffective. Despite these obstacles, the leaders of Fatah continued to launch attacks on Israel. At this stage the various Palestinian movements failed to unite under one main group and the PLO was discredited in the eyes of many Palestinians and Arabs. Eventually on 3 February 1969 Arafat was elected Chairman of the Executive Committee of the PLO. In the same year the American administration proposed a peace settlement. The Secretary of State, William Rogers, put forward a plan for an agreement between Israel on one side, and Egypt and Jordan on the other. The proposal included Israeli withdrawal as part of a package settlement, cessation of the state of war, secure and recognized borders, demilitarized zones and special arrangements in Gaza and Sharm al-Sheikh, freedom of navigation through the Straits of Tiran, Israel's use of the Suez Canal, and settlement of the refugee problem.

When the Egyptians agreed in principle to a modified revised peace agreement, the Palestinians unleashed a storm of protest among the resistance organizations in Jordan. Arafat and Fatah attacked Nasser; Nasser's response was to close down PLO broadcasting stations in Cairo and expel radical Palestinians from the country. During August and September, the situation in Jordan worsened. At this stage Arab mediators urged the PLO to compromise with Hussein. However, on 16 September 1970 martial law was declared and Hussein announced that he was setting up a military government to restore law and order as well as security. Within twenty-four hours fighting ensued in Amman as the army closed in on the Palestinian military personnel. Arafat attempted to speak to the king, but this proved impossible. Fighting intensified between the Palestinians and the Jordanian army. The Arab League sent a delegation to end the conflict. Eventually there was a fourteen-point agreement including a ceasefire and the withdrawal of all forces from Amman and their regrouping in agreed areas suitable for guerrilla attacks on Israel. Arafat maintained that Palestinian causalities numbered approximately 20,000, but according to the Red Cross the figure was probably around 3,000.

On 28 September 1970 Nasser died, and neither Hussein nor the Palestinians wished to carry out the agreement signed in Cairo. Hussein wanted all PLO fighters to leave Jordan. The Black September movement which was formed shortly afterwards was a Palestinian response to the shelling of the refugee camps in Amman which resulted in the death of men, women and children. The Palestinian poet Mahmoud Darwish expressed the feelings of desperation that drove subsequent acts of terrorism:

The one who has turned me into a refugee has made a bomb
   of me,
I know that I will die
I know that I am venturing into a lost battle today, because it is
   the battle of the future.
I know that Palestine on the map is far away from me
I know that you have forgotten its name and that you use a new
   name for it
I know all that
That is why I carry it to your streets, your homes, and your
   bedrooms
Palestine is not a land gentlemen of the jury
Palestine has become bodies that move
They move to the streets of the world, singing the song of death
Because the New Christ has given up his cross and gone out of
   Palestine.

(In Cohn-Sherbok and El-Alami,
The Palestine–Israel Conflict, p. 166)

Towards Liberation

After Palestinian freedom fighters left Jordan, it became apparent
that the Palestinian cause was losing support among Arab nations.
As far as Jordan was concerned, there were plans to create a new
united Arab kingdom, including the West Bank and Gaza, after
Israeli withdrawal. At the meeting of the Palestinian National Council in September 1972, President Sadat of Egypt urged the Palestinians to form a government in exile. Some time later the Egyptians
and Syrians launched a full-scale war against Israel: the October
War. Following these events, the UN General Assembly agreed on
Resolution 238 and negotiations began between Israel and Egypt to
disengage their forces.

In the mid-1970s the PLO and other Palestinian organizations
effectively controlled Lebanon. On 6 June 1982 the Israeli forces
pushed across Lebanon's border, supported by air and naval units.
Within eight days, the Israelis reached West Beirut, home to half a
million Lebanese and Palestinians and laid siege for more than two
months. The outcome was the exodus of the Palestinian fighters;

this led to the third exile for the Palestinians – and no armed Palestinians remained in Lebanon except for the refugees in the camps. In September 150 Christian Phalangists entered the camps of Sabra and Shatila, resulting in a massacre of approximately 2,000 refugees. As a result of the Israeli invasion of Lebanon, a total of approximately 40,000 Palestinians and Lebanese were killed, 100,000 were injured and 500,000 were made homeless. The major Palestinian political and social institutions were destroyed.

As a consequence the Palestinian political and armed freedom fighters were dispersed into the Arab world. The refugee camps, particularly in Lebanon, represented the depths of human misery and degradation, and their occupants were treated as prisoners and prevented from working to earn a living. No building materials were allowed into the camps and the refugees had to carry ID cards, which were renewed by the Lebanese authorities. There was no freedom of travel and violation of any administrative order would result in deportation or imprisonment. In the Occupied Territories, the situation was even more grave. A whole generation had been brought up under Israeli occupation to a life governed by barbed wire and an armed occupying force, military orders, restriction of movement, house demolitions, land confiscation, detention, deportation and other forms of degradation. New settlements were being constructed in the West Bank and Gaza, and Jewish immigration was increasing from throughout the world.

By the 1980s the mood in the Occupied Territories was one of simmering frustration. Palestinian anger boiled over and the *Intifada* was born. This was an uprising of the people, armed with stones and crude petrol bombs. Young boys with stones confronted Israeli soldiers with automatic weapons. The *Intifada* brought about a radical change within the PLO. At the nineteenth session of the Palestine National Council, which took place on 12–15 November 1988 in Algeria, Arafat proclaimed the creation of the State of Palestine with the holy city of Jerusalem as its capital, accepting Resolution 242 and 338. Up to this point, the PLO had denied the right of Israel to exist – no longer was this the Palestinian position.

By August 1988 a ceasefire had been implemented in the war between Iran and Iraq. Saddam Hussein was portraying this as an Iraqi victory, but the country was seriously damaged and depleted.

On 2 August 1990 the US issued an ultimatum to Baghdad to with-draw their forces from Kuwait. Arafat at this point threw in his lot with Saddam Hussein, believing that America would not attack and that the crisis would be resolved through negotiation between Arab countries. When the Iraqi forces were defeated in April 1991, Arafat and the PLO were left (along with Jordan and Yemen) sepa-rated from the majority of Arab countries that had been against the Iraqi invasion. The PLO lost the financial support of Saudi Arabia and Kuwait, and large numbers of Palestinians were forced out of these countries; many settled in Jordan.

On 6 March 1991 President Bush stated that a comprehensive peace plan must be grounded in Resolutions 242 and 338, and in the principle of territory for peace. On October of the same year, James Baker met with a group of prominent Palestinians in the Occupied Territories. One of the central difficulties was to find a way to make Palestinians and Israelis meet together. Eventually an agreement was reached whereby the Palestinians would be repre-sented by a Jordanian–Palestinian delegation and the PLO would be excluded. As a compromise the Palestinians would be permitted to choose the members of the Palestinian delegation, and Israel was to have no veto. Yet the Israelis refused to meet certain members of the Palestinian delegation. The aim of these talks was to reach an agreement within a year on arrangements for a five-year interim period during which negotiations were to begin about permanent status on the basis of the UN Resolutions.

The Madrid Conference was attended by the Palestinian delega-tion, a number of prominent Arab leaders, President Bush and the Israeli Prime Minister Yitzhak Shamir. The central achievement of the Madrid Conference was that Arabs and Israelis sat at the same negotiating table. Madrid established a two-track system which became the pattern for subsequent negotiations. The first track was the multilateral negotiations in which Israel, the Palestinians and the Arab states as well as other parties could join in discussion; the second track was the bilateral track in which Israel negotiated in Washington with each of its Arab neighbours. Yet recognition of the PLO remained a problem. On 9 September 1993, Arafat sent a letter to Prime Minister Rabin confirming that the PLO recog-nized the State of Israel, was committed to the peace process and renounced the use of terrorism and other acts of violence. Further, he affirmed that those Articles of the Palestinian covenant that denied Israel's right to exist were inoperative. Rabin responded by outlining that the government of Israel had decided to recognize the PLO as the representative of the Palestinian people and that it would commence negotiation with the PLO.

Despite such developments, the PLO remained subordinate, with Israel still in charge of East Jerusalem, the settlements, sovereignty and the economy. By August 1995 negotiations were under way in Eilat in an attempt to press ahead with the peace process. The same year the Oslo II agreement was signed in Washington, and Israeli forces began to withdraw from six West Bank cities. Yet the Palestinians felt that these agreements offered little: the issue of land and settlements had not been discussed. Only a few months later Rabin was assassinated, and Palestinian leaders feared that Shimon Peres might not be able to enforce the agreement for Palestinian self-rule if he became prime minister. When Benjamin Netanyahu was elected instead, the Israeli government reversed the previous policy and the hopes of the Palestinians for the creation of an independent Palestinian state in the West Bank and Gaza were shattered. Instead, Netanyahu allowed further expansion of the settlements.

The Quest for Statehood

The next stage in Israeli–Palestinian negotiations took place at the Wye River Conference Centre in Maryland. After nine days of meetings, President Clinton invited Yasser Arafat and Prime Minister Netanyahu to the White House to sign an agreement. The essence of the treaty was the strengthening of Israeli security, expansion of the area of Palestinian control in the West Bank, and enhancement of the opportunities for Israeli and Palestinian people alike. Yet the Palestinians believed that little had been accomplished since the Palestinian National Authority had the trappings but not the substance of government.

No further progress was made until the government of Israeli Prime Minister Netanyahu fell, and Ehud Barak and the Labour Party were elected. This gave fresh hope that the peace process could be reignited. On 4 September 1999 an agreement was signed by the Prime Minister of Israel and Arafat in the presence of Egypt and Jordan to implement the Wye River Agreement. The next day the Sharm al-Sheikh agreement was signed which dealt with a wide range of issues including the Israeli withdrawal from Palestinian areas. Throughout the year, and into 2000, negotiations on the implementation of the land for peace proposals of the Wye Agreements failed repeatedly. By the middle of 2000 it was becoming clear that no acceptable solution was going to be reached. In the Palestinian view, Israel as the occupying power continued to dictate terms to the Palestinians. The obstacle to a peace agreement was the Israeli presence in the Occupied Territories. The mood of the Palestinians was one of simmering anger at the hopelessness of their situation and despair of there ever being a just solution. Like the first *Intifada*, the uprising of the Palestinian people was a spontaneous reaction. In small acts of defiance, ordinary Palestinians expressed their frustration in the form of demonstrations, strikes and episodes of symbolic stone-throwing by gangs of youths. Suicide bombings heightened this stage of animosity further and generated sympathy for Israel as a victim of terrorism, providing it with ammunition against the Palestinians.

In the ensuing years, divisions among the Palestinians themselves made any kind of united front impossible and undermined their credibility. In Gaza, in particular, there had long been deeply rooted dissatisfaction with Fatah. Meanwhile, Hamas was active on the ground, using its organizational expertise to help to provide welfare and services including schools and medical clinics. In 2006, Hamas candidates standing as the 'List for Change and Reform' won 72 out of 132 seats. In the following months, attempts to bring about some form of coalition between Hamas and Fatah failed and a state of hostility between the two groups prevailed. Hamas gained overall control of Gaza and the response of Israel was effectively to close the Gaza Strip, Western aid to Gaza being cut off. As a consequence, Gaza descended into a state of near third-world poverty and deprivation with humanitarian agencies reporting malnutrition and an impending humanitarian disaster. Fatah retained control of the West Bank, but this situation was severely curtailed by the separation fence that was constructed across the country. Much longer than the border it claimed to secure, it wound its way around towns and villages, strangling the economy and devastating communities and local agriculture.

Since early 2007 there have been new externally sponsored peace initiatives. In February 2007 talks were convened between US Secretary of State Condolezza Rice, Ehud Olmert and Mahmoud Abbas, but little was accomplished. The promise offered by the peace negotiations of the nineties faded. At the beginning of 2008 George W. Bush visited Jerusalem as part of a tour of several countries in the Middle East. He expressed the US commitment to Israel and also pledged support for the Palestinians in their aspirations for a state of their own. He urged Palestinians to oppose extremism and terrorism as the greatest threats to their aspirations. Meanwhile in Gaza, still blockaded and sliding into a humanitarian crisis, the situation became increasingly grave, leading eventually to armed conflict.

Since his election as US president, Barack Obama has attempted to rekindle peace negotiations between Israel and the Palestinians. On 4 June 2009 he delivered a speech at Cairo University which called for improved mutual understanding and relations between the Islamic world and the West. While reaffirming America's alliance with Israel, he described Palestinian statelessness as intolerable. This was followed by a series of meetings between Israeli and Palestinian representatives. Yet direct talks broke down in September 2010 when an Israeli partial moratorium on settlement construction in the West Bank expired. Prime Minister Netanyahu refused to extend the freeze unless the Palestinian leadership recognized Israel as a Jewish state while the Palestinian leadership refused to continue negotiating unless Israel extended the moratorium. In the view of the Palestinians, the topic of the Jewishness of the state had nothing to do with the building freeze. On 16 January 2011 another setback for the peace process took place when Israel accepted a plan to build over 1,000 more homes in Jerusalem.

In reaction to the attempt to restart the peace process, on 29 October 2010 tens of thousands of Islamic Jihad supporters demonstrated in Gaza City against negotiations and making peace with Israel. Shouting 'Death to America' and 'Death to Israel', they were convinced that making peace with Israel would only bring war and destruction to the area. One of their leaders, Mohammad al-Hindi, called for an end to the Palestinian Authority, declaring that Jihad

was the fate of the nation. In the view of leading Islamic Jihad officials, the turnout was a referendum by the Palestinian people reject-
ing the peace-making process with Israel. According to Hams leader
Khali Al-Hayya, there is only one choice: Jihad and nothing else.

More recently, Israeli and Palestinian negotiators failed to make a
breakthrough at their first high-level discussions on 3 January 2012
in Jordan. The talks were aimed at agreeing terms under which
President Mahmoud Abbas and Israeli Prime Minister Netanyahu
could hold talks. Prior to the meeting, Palestinian negotiator Saeb
Erekat said that he did not know if the Israelis were bringing anything new to the discussion or if they were willing to put their position on the table. A senior figure on the PLO executive claimed that
Israel and the Palestinians were simply fulfilling a request by the
'Quartet' of Middle East mediators (the United States, the European Union, Russia and the United Nations) to present their positions on security and borders. Before the talks, Mahmoud Abbas
stated that Palestinians could take unilateral steps if Israel did not
agree to halt settlement building in the occupied West Bank and
recognize the borders of a future Palestinian state. Following this
meeting, it was agreed that the two sides had until 25 January 2012
to make progress, and that meetings would take place in Jordan on
a continual basis without prior announcement of time and date.

Summary

The pogroms of Eastern Europe in 1881–1882 forced many Jews
to emigrate; most went to the United States but a sizeable number
settled in Palestine. A decade later the idea of Jewish nationalism
spread to various countries in Europe. For these early Zionists the
only solution to the problem of antisemitism was the establishment
of a Jewish state in Palestine. From the beginning of the twentieth
century onwards the indigenous Arab population became increasingly alarmed by what they considered to be an illegitimate influx of
colonialist foreigners. Determined to protect what they perceived as
their inalienable rights, they sought by whatever means to expel an
alien population. The blood-soaked history of the Middle East testi-
fies to the Palestinian quest for independence and sovereignty over
their own country.

Chapter 6
Towards a Palestinian State

Aware of Zionist aspirations, Palestinian Arabs were bitterly opposed to an influx of Jews settling in what they perceived as their native soil. These foreign immigrants were regarded as usurpers of their native land. Partition was therefore categorically rejected. In recent years, however, the Palestinians have pressed for a two-state solution which would grant them Palestinian statehood, and negotiations between the Israeli government and the Palestinian leadership have been directed toward this end.

Early Proposals

Faced with the growing threat of Nazism, Zionist leaders were determined to create a Jewish state as quickly as possible. In the view of leading Zionists, it was necessary to save European Jewry at any cost even if it meant abandoning the quest to create a Jewish homeland throughout the whole of the country. Such considerations persuaded Zionist leaders in 1936–1937 to agree to the concept of partition as outlined by the Peel Commission. As we noted, the commissioners recommended that the Mandate be dissolved and approximately 20 per cent of Palestine (the Galilee and the northern and central sectors of the Coastal Plain) be assigned

to the Jews. The rest of the country was to be under Arab control. It was envisaged that eventually the Arab area would be transferred to Jordan to create a Greater Jordan under the rule of the
Hashemite Prince Abdullah. The remaining 5–10 per cent of the
country, including Jerusalem and Bethlehem, was set aside for British rule. The Peel Commission also recommended the transfer of
hundreds of thousands of Arabs who were living on the Jewish side
of the partition areas to neighbouring Arab states.The Peel proposals, however, were rejected by the Palestine Arab leadership as well
as by Arabs outside Palestine. By May 1939, the British had abandoned the concept of partition as well as Jewish statehood, envis-
aging the emergence of a Palestinian state governed by the Arab
majority of the country.

Ten years later the United Nations Special Committee on Palestine (UNSCOP) examined the ongoing conflict in the area. The
seven-member majority (Sweden, Czechoslovakia, Guatemala, the
Netherlands, Canada, Peru and Uruguay) recommended the partition of Palestine into two states. The Jewish state was to have
about 60 per cent of the land; the Arab state was to to have about
40 per cent. The Jerusalem–Bethlehem area was to be internation-
alized. The Australian member of UNSCOP abstained. But the
three remaining members (India, Yugoslavia and Iran) submitted a
minority report recommending a one-state solution which would be
governed by the majority of its inhabitants. On the basis of the UN
General Assembly's endorsement of partition, David Ben-Gurion
read out Israel's Declaration of Independence on 14 May 1948.

In the post-1948 period, partition became a reality. The Jews
retained 8,000 square miles of Israel while the Arabs ruled the rest
of Palestine, which consisted of 2,000 square miles on the West
Bank with East Jerusalem and the Gaza Strip. As Benny Morris
noted in *One State, Two States*:

> The official policy of the successive Labor-led Israeli govern-
> ments, under Ben-Gurion (1949–1953), Moshe Sharett (1953–
> 1955), again Ben-Gurion (1955–1963), and then Levi Eshkol
> (from 1963) was to allow the territorial partition that resulted
> from the clash of arms in 1948 to stay. Indeed no effort was
> made by Israel to exploit this or that local bout of hostilities to

annex the West Bank or even the Gaza Strip (even though, in
the wake of the 1956 Sinai–Suez War, when Israel conquered
the Sinai Peninsula and the Gaza Strip, Jerusalem made an
unsuccessful diplomatic effort to block the Egyptian army's
return to Gaza).

(Morris, *One State, Two States*, pp. 80–81)

The Six-Day War fundamentally altered this division of land. In
its war with Egypt, Jordan and Syria, Israeli forces overran the
West Bank, East Jerusalem and the Gaza Strip in addition to the
Sinai Peninsula and the Golan Heights. This victory, which was
celebrated throughout Israel, marked a return to the central north-
south spine of the country which the Israeli army had failed to con-
quer in 1948. As Moshe Dayan remarked:

We have returned to the hill(s), to the cradle of our people's
history, to the land of the patriarchs, the land of the Judges and
the stronghold of the Kingdom of the House of David. We have
returned to Hebron [the site of the tombs of Patriarchs Abraham, Isaac and Jacob, and their wives, and King David's first
capital] . . . to Bethlehem [King David's birthplace] and Anatto
[the birthplace of Jeremiah], to Jericho [the town conquered by
the Israelite tribes as they entered Canaan under Joshua] and
the fords of the Jordan at the city of Adam.

(Quoted in Naor, 'Greater Israel', p. 9, in Morris,
One State, Two States, pp. 81–82)

In Israel, opinions were divided about such an expansion of the
state. Religious Zionists viewed the victory as part of God's provi-
dential plan for his chosen people. Many secular Jews embraced
the notion of a Greater Israel. Nonetheless, on 19 June the Israeli
cabinet resolved to hand back Sinai and the Golan Heights to
Egypt and Syria in exchange for peace, but no decision was reached
about the West Bank. Humiliated by defeat, the Arab League at its
Summit in Khartoum in September refused to consider such a plan.
In July–August 1967 General Allon presented a plan to retain the
majority of the land of Israel while giving up the hilly spine of
the country including Hebron, Bethlehem, Ramallah, Nablus and

Jenin. This scheme envisaged handing back the hill country of the northern and southern segments of the West Bank to Jordan while retaining East Jerusalem and a stretch of the southern Jordan Valley west of the river along with the whole western shoreline of the Dead Sea. Allon was reluctant to hand over the core of the West Bank to the Palestinians, fearing it could serve as a basis for future attack on Israel.

In essence the Allon plan reverted to the Peel Commission's recommendations, endorsing a two-state solution but with the Arabs retaining less of Palestine, which would consist of 70–90 per cent of the West Bank. The cabinet, however, refused to endorse Allon's scheme, and the concept of a two-state solution to the problems of the Middle East was temporarily abandoned.

The Two-State Solution

It was not until the 1970s that the PLO indicated its willingness to consider a two-state solution to the problems of the Middle East. Such a view was expressed by Said Hammami. The Security Council Resolutions supporting such a concept based on the pre-1967 borders date back to June 1976. Yet, these were vetoed by the United States, which insisted that any borders had to be negotiated by both Israel and the Palestinians. Since the 1970s the UN General Assembly, expressed its overwhelming support for such a scheme. Later, on 15 November 1988, the Palestinians issued a Declaration of Independence which referred to the UN Partition Plan of 1947 as well as UN Resolutions issued since 1946. These pronouncements were regarded as an indirect recognition of the State of Israel and support for a two-state resolution.

The Declaration itself was written by the Palestinian poet Mahmoud Darwish and proclaimed by Yasser Arafat. Previously it had been adopted by the Palestinian National Council, the legislative body of the PLO. It was read at the closing session of the 19th Palestinian National Council; upon completing its reading, Arafat as Chairman of the Palestine Liberation Organization assumed the title of 'President of Palestine'. The Declaration itself concerned the Palestine region as defined by the British Mandate, which included the whole of Israel as well as the West Bank and the Gaza Strip.

The document referred back to the United Nations plan for the Partition of Palestine in 1947, which Israel had used as the basis for its legitimacy as well as various UN Resolutions. This partition plan was envisaged as providing legitimacy to Palestinian statehood. Although the Declaration did not explicitly recognize the State of Israel, an accompanying document did mention Security Council Resolution 242 which implies the recognition of a Jewish state. This Resolution refers to the inadmissibility of the acquisition of territory by war and the need to work for a just and lasting peace in the Middle East in which every state can live in security. The Resolution goes on to advocate two central principles:

(1) Withdrawal of Israel armed forces from territories occupied in the recent conflict.
(2) Termination of all claims or states of belligerency and respect for and acknowledgement of the sovereignty, territorial integrity and political independence of every State in the area and their right to live in peace within secure and recognized boundaries free from threats of acts of force.

In addition, the accompanying document refers to Yasser Arafat's statements in Geneva a month later, which were interpreted by the United States as sufficient to remove any ambiguities about acknowledging Israel's right to exist in the Declaration itself.

On the basis of such an interpretation, the Palestinian Declaration appears to recognize the State of Israel in line with the pre-1967 borders. In the past Zionists were viewed by the Palestinians as usurpers who had displaced the indigenous population. Here was a clear change in perspective. Nonetheless, the Declaration emphasized the historical injustice inflicted on the Palestinians, resulting in their dispersion and depriving them of the right to self-determination. In support of this view, the document refers to the Treaty of Lausanne of 1923 and UN General Assembly Resolution 181 as support for Palestinian rights. The Declaration went on to proclaim Palestine as a state with its capital in Jerusalem. Although the borders of the state were not specified, the population was referred to by the claim that the State of Palestine is an Arab state, an integral and indivisible part of the Arab nation.

The Declaration was accompanied by a call for multilateral negotiations on the basis of the UN Security Council Resolution 242. The Palestinian National Council's political communiqué accompanying the Declaration called for a withdrawal from Arab Jerusalem as well as other Occupied Territories. As a result of the Declaration, the United Nations General Assembly convened, inviting Yasser Arafat as Chairman of the PLO to give an address. In addition, a United Nations General Assembly resolution was adopted which acknowledged the proclamation of the State of Palestine, and it was agreed that the designation 'Palestine' should be used in place of the designation 'Palestine Liberation Organization' in the United Nations itself. Over a hundred states voted for this resolution; 44 abstained, and the United Nations and Israel voted against. By mid-December, 75 states had recognized the State of Palestine; by February 1989 the number had increased to 93.

Increasingly, both Palestinians and Israelis as well as the Arab League were prepared to accept a two-state solution to the Middle East problem. During the 1990s considerable efforts were made in this regard, beginning with the Oslo Accords which were officially referred to as the Declaration of Principles on Interim Self-Government Arrangements or Declaration of Principles. This was the first direct face-to-face agreement between Israel and the PLO, and was intended to serve as à framework for future negotiations. As an outgrowth of the Madrid Conference of 1991 the meeting was conducted in secret in Oslo, Norway. Negotiations were concluded on 20 August 1993, and the Accords were publicly signed at a ceremony in Washington on 13 September 1993 in the presence of Yasser Arafat, Israeli Prime Minister Yitzhak Rabin and US President Bill Clinton. The documents themselves were signed by Mahmoud Abbas for the PLO and Israeli foreign minister Shimon Peres as well as US Secretary of State Warren Christopher and Russian Foreign Minister Andrei Kozyrev.

The Oslo Accords provided for the creation of a Palestinian National Authority (PNA) which was to be given responsibility for the administration of the territory under its control. The Accords also called for the withdrawal of the Israel Defense Forces from parts of the Gaza Strip and the West Bank. It was intended that this arrangement would last for a five-year interim period during which a permanent agreement would be negotiated not later than May 1996. Major issues including Jerusalem, Palestinian refugees, Israeli settlement, and security and borders were to determined at a later date – Israel was to grant interim Palestinian self-determination in phases. Along with the principles, Israel and the Palestinians signed Letters of Mutual Recognition: the Israeli government recognized the PLO as the legitimate representative of the Palestinian people; the PLO recognized the right of Israel to exist and renounced terrorism as well as other forms of violence. The five-year period was to commence with an Israeli withdrawal from the Gaza Strip and Jericho. Permanent status negotiations were to begin as soon as possible so that the negotiators would be able to explore the central issues facing both Israel and the Palestinians. Both sides agreed on a division of their respective jurisdictions in the West Bank into areas A and B (Palestinian jurisdiction), and area C (Israeli jurisdiction). It was envisaged that there would be a transfer of authority from the Israel Defense Forces to authorized Palestinians concerning education, culture, health, social welfare, taxation and tourism. It was accepted that the Palestinian Council would create a police force while Israel would continue to have responsibility for defending the country against external threats. Finally, an Israeli–Palestinian Economic Cooperation Committee would be established to develop and implement the programmes identified in the protocols.

Continuing Negotiations

On 5 July 2000, President Clinton announced his intention to invite Israeli Prime Minister Ehud Barak and Yasser Arafat to a summit at Camp David to continue their discussions. On 11 July 2000 the meetings began but ended on 25 July without an agreement being reached. However, a Trilateral Statement was issued. Although the two leaders were unable to bridge the gaps between their positions, they agreed on a number of principles:

(1) The two sides agreed that the aim of their negotiations was to put an end to the conflict between Israeli and the Palestinians and create a just and lasting peace.

(2) The two sides committed themselves to continue their efforts to conclude an agreement on all permanent status issues.
(3) There was an agreement that negotiations based on UN Security Council Resolutions 242 and 338 should serve as a framework for a future agreement.
(4) The two sides stressed the importance of avoiding unilateral actions that would prejudice the outcome of future discussions.
(5) It was agreed that the United States is a vital partner in the search for peace.

In their discussions, there were several key obstacles to reaching an agreement. First, the Palestinian negotiators demanded that there should be full Palestinian sovereignty over the entire West Bank and the Gaza Strip. In their view, Resolution 242 called for full Israeli withdrawal from those areas which were captured in the Six-Day War. In the 1993 Oslo Accords the Palestinians had accepted the Green Line borders for the West Bank, but the Israelis had rejected this proposal. Instead, they wished to annex numerous settlement blocks on the Palestinian side of the Green Line, fearing that a return to the 1967 borders could constitute a threat to Israeli security.

Prime Minister Barak offered to create a Palestinian state on 73 percent of the West Bank (27 percent less than the Green Line Borders), and 100 percent of the Gaza Strip. It was envisaged that in 10–25 years the Palestinian state would expand to a maximum of 90–91 percent of the West Bank. As a consequence, Israel would have withdrawn from 63 settlements; Israel would keep only the settlements with large populations. All others would be dismantled with the exception of Kiryat Arba, which would serve as an Israeli enclave inside the Palestinian state. The West Bank would be split in the middle by an Israeli-controlled road from Jerusalem to the Dead Sea with free passage to the Palestinians. Israel would permit the Palestinians to use a highway in the Negev to connect the West Bank with Gaza. According to this proposal, the West Bank and Gaza would be linked by an elevated highway and an elevated railroad, under the sovereignty of Israel, which could be closed in the case of an emergency. The Palestinians, however, rejected this proposal on the grounds that Israel did not offer land in return for the land it wished to annex. Further, the settlements that Israel sought to annex cut existing road networks between population centres, and the settlement blocs that Israel wished to keep separated the West Bank into cantons. For the Palestinians it was unacceptable that Israel could control freedom of movement inside a Palestinian state.

A second issue concerned Jerusalem and the Temple Mount. Barak told his delegates to view this topic as the central issue that would decide the destiny of the negotiations; Arafat insisted that his delegation would not compromise. The Palestinians demanded that they should have complete sovereignty over East Jerusalem and its holy sites. In their view, all of East Jerusalem should be handed back, but the Jewish Quarter and the Western Wall should be placed under Israel authority rather than its sovereignty. Israel, on the other hand, proposed that the Palestinians should be granted custodianship rather than sovereignty of the Temple Mount while Israel retained control over the Western Wall. In addition, the Israeli delegation recommended that the Palestinians be granted administration rather than sovereignty over the Muslim and Christian Quarters of the Old City with the Jewish and Armenian Quarters staying under Israeli control (the Israelis were prepared to accede to Palestinian sovereignty over the Muslim and Christian Quarters). The Palestinians would be granted administrative control over all Islamic and Christian holy sites and allowed to raise the Palestinian flag over them. The Israeli team also proposed annexing to Israel Jerusalem settlements within the West Bank beyond the Green Line; it was also suggested that the Palestinians merge together certain outer Arab villages and small cities that had been annexed to Jerusalem after 1967 to create a capital of Palestine. Israeli neighbourhoods within East Jerusalem would remain under Israeli sovereignty. Outlying Arab neighbourhoods in Jerusalem would come under Palestinian sovereignty and core Arab neighbourhoods would remain under Israeli sovereignty but would gain autonomous powers. Finally, Palestinian Jerusalem would be run by a Palestinian civilian administration with the possibility of merging it to Israeli Jerusalem, in which case Palestinian Jerusalem would be governed by a Palestinian branch municipality within the framework of an Israeli higher municipal council. The Palestinians objected to the lack of sovereignty in such proposals, and also rejected the notion that Israel would retain sovereignty over culturally and religiously significant Arab neighbourhoods in Jerusalem. They were also disturbed by the suggestion that Israel would have the right to keep Jewish neighbourhoods that it had constructed over the Green Line in East Jerusalem.

There was also significant disagreement concerning the rights of the approximately four million Palestinian refugees. Since the time of the first Arab–Israeli war, the Palestinians have demanded the right of return and the restoration of property or compensation. Repeatedly the Israeli government has argued that such a large number of refugees would overwhelm the country and fundamentally alter the nature of Israeli society. At Camp David the Palestinians continued to insist that the right of return be implemented. So as not fundamentally to alter Israeli life, the Palestinians promised that the right to return would be implemented by a formula agreed by both sides, which would channel a large number of refugees away from the option of returning to their ancestral home. Nonetheless, each refugee would have the right to return to Israel. It was envisaged that the Palestinians who chose to return to Israel would do so gradually with Israel absorbing 150,000 refugees a year. The Israeli negotiators, concerned that such an influx would undermine the character of the Jewish state, therefore proposed that a maximum of 100,000 refugees should be allowed entry. All other Palestinian refugees should be settled in their current place of residence (either other countries or a Palestinian state), and Israel would help fund their absorption. In this regard an international fund of $30 billion would be established to which Israel along with other countries would contribute in order to provide compensation for property lost by Palestinian refugees.

The final issue concerned Israeli security. The Israeli negotiators proposed that Israel be permitted to construct radar stations inside the Palestinian state and be allowed to use its airspace. Israel also wished to have the right to deploy troops on Palestinian territory under certain conditions. It was also recommended that an international force should be stationed in the Jordan valley. Palestinian authorities would maintain control of border crossings under temporary Israeli observation. Israel should also be allowed to maintain a permanent security presence along 15 per cent of the Palestinian-Jordanian border. Israel also insisted that the Palestinian state be demilitarized with the exception of a paramilitary security force; it should also not make alliances without Israeli approval or allow the introduction of foreign forces east of the Jordan River. It was also to dismantle terrorist groups. The Israelis also wanted water resources on the West Bank to be made available to both sides. Finally, Israel insisted that Arafat declare that the Middle East conflict had ended, and make no further demands.

Further Steps

Following the Camp David meeting, negotiations continued in Taba, Egypt, in January 2001, but no final agreement was reached. In 2002, Crown Prince Abdullah of Saudi Arabia proposed the Arab Peace Initiative, which was supported unanimously by the Arab League. During this period President George W. Bush gave his support for a Palestinian state; this opened the way for United Nations Council Resolution 1397, which supported a two-state solution. At the Annapolis Conference in November 2007 the Palestinians, represented solely by Fatah (excluding the Hamas government in Gaza), the Israelis and the Americans agreed on a two-state solution as the framework for negotiation.

Since Barack Obama became President of the United States in January 2009, he stated that a peace settlement between Israel and the Palestinians should be a major priority. In March 2009, US Secretary of State Hillary Rodham Clinton went to Israel. At this time she stated that Israel settlements and the demolition of Arab homes in East Jerusalem hindered the peace process. She also voiced her support for the creation of a Palestinian state. Prime Minister designate Benjamin Netanyahu expressed his support for Palestinian self-government but did not endorse the US and Palestinian vision of statehood. When the Obama administration's special envoy, George Mitchell, arrived in Israel, Netanyahu stated that any furtherance of negotiations with the Palestinians would be conditional on the Palestinians recognizing Israel as a Jewish state. Up to this point, the Palestinian leadership rejected a US-backed proposal extending a settlement freeze in exchange for recognizing Israel.

On 4 June 2009, President Barack Obama delivered an address which supported a two-state solution to the Muslim world in Cairo. For decades, he stated, there has been a stalemate. Two peoples with legitimate aspirations, each with a painful history that makes compromise elusive. It is easy to point fingers, he continued, for Palestinians to point to the displacement brought by Israel's founding, and for Israelis to point to the constant hostility and attacks throughout its history from within its borders as well as beyond. But if we see this conflict from only one side or the other, then we will be blind to the truth: the only resolution is for the aspirations of both sides to be met through two states.

In response to Obama, on 14 June Netanyahu gave a speech at Bar IIan University in which he endorsed a demilitarized Palestinian state after two months of refusing to commit anything other than self-ruling autonomy. In his speech he declared that United Jerusalem is the capital of the Jewish people and the State of Israel. Israeli sovereignty was non-negotiable. He went on to state that if such a state were to be established, the Palestinians should have no military and they would have to abandon their demand for a right of return. He also claimed that there should be natural growth in the existing settlements in the West Bank, while their permanent status should be subject to further negotiation.

The following month, on 12 July 2009, Mahmoud Abbas told Egyptian media that he would not abandon any part of the West Bank to Israel, that he would demand territorial contiguity between the West Bank and the Gaza Strip, and that he would never waive the Palestinian right of return. In a letter to President Obama he maintained that any peace deal should be based on the 1967 borders. The Palestinian negotiator, Saeb Erekat, rejected any middle-ground solution, stating that the Palestinians would reject any deal between the US and Israel that would allow construction to continue in Israeli settlements.

On 23 August 2009, Netanyahu announced in his weekly cabinet meeting that negotiations between Israel and the Palestinians would begin the following month and would be officially launched on his forthcoming visit to New York after he accepted an invitation from President Barack Obama for a summit there. On the same day Mahmoud Abbas stated that there would be no negotiations as long as Israel continued its settlement construction. On 20 September 2009 the White House announced that it would host a three-way meeting between President Obama, Prime Minister Netanyahu, and PA President Mahmoud Abbas within the framework of the United Nations General Assembly to establish a basis for renewed negotiations for a peaceful settlement of the Middle East conflict.

Two months later, on 25 November 2009, Israel imposed a 10-month construction freeze on all its settlements in the West Bank. However, it continued its construction of 3000 pre-approved housing units in the West Bank and did not extend the freeze to East Jerusalem. Israel's decision was widely viewed as the result of pressure from the United States administration. In his announcement, Netanyahu referred to this initiative as a painful step that would encourage the peace process and called upon the Palestinians to respond positively. In response, the Palestinian Authority rejected the partial freeze and refused to enter negotiations.

Nearly a year later, on 31 May 2010, relations between Israel and the Palestinians became further strained when Israel carried out the Gaza flotilla raid. The flotilla was organized by the Free Gaza Movement and the Turkish Foundation for Human Rights and Freedoms and Humanitarian Relief. Its aim was to bring about humanitarian aid and construction materials with the intention of breaking the Israeli–Egyptian blockade of the Gaza Strip. Israeli naval commandos boarded the ships from speedboats and helicopters. In the ensuing confrontation with one of the ships, nine activists were killed and many others wounded; ten Israeli commandos were also injured. The raid drew widespread criticism internationally. Eventually Israel eased its blockade on the Gaza Strip; all activists were freed; and the ships returned. Responding to these events, Mahmoud Abbas stated that Israel had committed a massacre and declared a three-day mourning period.

On 8 July 2010, Abbas told the Arab League that the Palestinian Authority would abandon peace talks and attack Israel if the Arab states were also to invade. The next month Barack Obama and Hilary Clinton stated that the establishment of a Palestine state could be achieved within a year, and renewed efforts were made to negotiate peace. In this quest Obama obtained support for direct talks from Egypt and Jordan who persuaded the Palestinian leadership to accept Israel's settlement freeze and enter direct talks. The aim of such meetings would be to forge the framework of a final agreement for a two-state solution by the end of the year.

Towards a Solution

After many months, direct negotiations began between Israel and the Palestinian Authority in Washington DC on 2 September 2010. Nearly two weeks later a second round of Middle East talks concluded in Sharm el-Sheikh, Egypt. According to Mahmoud Abbas, during the meetings the Palestinian Authority and Israel agreed on the principle of land swap; Israel was to exchange small parts of its territory for border settlement blocs. The issue of the ratio of land Israel would hand over to the Palestinians in exchange for border settlement blocs was problematic – the Palestinians demanded that the ratio be 1:1, but Israel offered less.

During the meetings that took place between Israel and the Palestinians, Hamas and Hezbollah were determined to threaten the peace talks if both sides reached a firm agreement. Thirteen militant groups led by Hamas began a campaign to disrupt the peace process, and in a series of attacks eight Israelis were wounded. On 21 September, Palestinian Minister Salam Fayyad left a meeting in New York which was held as part of the ad-hoc Liaison Committee meetings, cancelled a press conference with Israeli President Simon Peres and Deputy Foreign Minister Danny Ayalon following Ayalon's demand that the summary of the meeting refer to the notion of two states for two peoples, implying that Israel should be seen as a Jewish state alongside a Palestinian state (rather than a Palestinian state alongside a bi-national Israel). Despite such conflict, in a speech to the United Nations two days later President Obama indicated that he was hopeful of a diplomatic peace within one year.

As the 10-month freeze on settlement construction was nearing its end on 26 September, Mahmoud Abbas declared that he would abandon the negotiations if settlement construction were renewed. Israel, he stated, has a moratorium for months, and it should be extended to three to four months more to give peace a chance. The Palestinian Authority leadership regarded Israel's construction of settlements as an imposition of facts of in the ground in the West Bank and a violation of international law. During this period the Israeli Knesset passed a law requiring a public referendum and the votes of at least 60 Knesset members ahead of any withdrawal from East Jerusalem or the Golan Heights. On 25 September – a day before the expiration of the freeze – Abbas maintained in the United Nations General Assembly that Israeli settlements constituted a central issue. Israel, he said, must choose between peace and the continuation of such construction.

In the face of Palestinian and international pressure to extend the freeze, on 26 September Netanyahu called on West Bank settlers to show restraint following the end of the freeze. At the same time a number of Israeli right-wing politicians urged the settlers to resume building. The Israeli Foreign Minister, Avigdor Lieberman, refuted the view that the renewal of West Bank settlement construction was intended to undermine the peace process; in his view the Palestinians had failed to accept the gesture of a moratorium for nine months. Instead, they were attempting to pressurize Israel to continue the freeze. Israel, he said, was willing to continue peace talks but without preconditions. Nonetheless, he ruled out the idea that a Palestinian state would be created within two years.

Israel's determination not to extend the moratorium was widely criticized. Mahmoud Abbas stated that Prime Minister Netanyahu could not be trusted as a genuine negotiator. On 2 October 2010 he stated that peace negotiations would not continue until Israel imposed a new freeze on the construction of settlements in the West Bank. Two days later Netanyahu claimed that the Israelis were working behind the scenes with the United States to resume talks. Israeli ambassador to the United Nations, Michael Oren, stated that the United States had offered Israel incentives for an extension to the freeze. At this stage Chief Palestinian negotiator Nail Shaath accepted a US proposal to extend the West Bank settlement freeze for another two months. In his view, the Palestinians would be prepared to accept such a timescale as long as the two sides could reach an agreement on the borders between Israel and a Palestinian state within these two months.

On 8 October at a meeting in Libya the Arab League leaders announced their support for the Palestinian Authority President's decision to halt peace talks, stating that it would give the United States a further month to persuade Israel to renew the moratorium. On 11 October Prime Minster Netanyahu in a speech at the opening of the Knesset offered a settlement freeze if the Palestinian Authority would declare its recognition of Israel as the homeland of the Jewish people. This suggestion was rejected by the Palestinian Authority. According to Mahmoud Abbas, the Palestinians would never sign an agreement recognising Israel as a Jewish state. Speaking on behalf of the Palestinian Authority, chief negotiator Saeb Erekat declared that the PA rejects what he regarded as the racist demands of the Israelis. As the Palestinian negotiators explained, recognition of Israel as a Jewish state would undermine the rights of Israeli Arabs and eliminate the right of return for millions of Palestinian refugees. Four days later it was reported that Israel had approved new construction in East Jerusalem.

During this period Yasser Abed Rabbo, the secretary general of the PLO, declared in a press statement that the PLO would recognize Israel as a Jewish state in exchange for a sovereign Palestinian state within the 1967 borders including East Jerusalem. Yet his statement was immediately disowned by various Palestinian factions since his remarks were viewed as conceding the right of return for Palestinian refugees. The Fatah movement called for Rabbo's resignation. Palestinian negotiator Nail Shaath dismissed Rabbo's statement and claimed that they did not reflect the views of either the PLO or the Fatah movement. The Hamas government in Gaza also called for Rabbo's resignation.

In November 2010 the US government offered Israel the incentive of a 3 billion dollar package including the delivery of 20 F-35s, various missile and layered defence systems to agree to a 90-day freeze on settlement construction in the West Bank excluding East Jerusalem. In addition, the US promised to veto the UN Security Council resolution relating to the peace process during the negotiating period and would not ask Israel to extend the 90-day moratorium when it expired. The Israeli Security Cabinet considered the offer. However, Mahmoud Abbas rejected the US freeze proposal since it did not include East Jerusalem, and Saeb Erekat restated the Palestinian demand for unconditional recognition of the 1967 borders and a withdrawal from East Jerusalem.

On 2 December a Palestinian official announced that Washington had officially informed the PA that Israel had refused to agree to a freeze on its settlements. Nonetheless, Defense Minister Ehud Barak attempted to restart negotiations by imposing a de facto settlement freeze blocking building plans in the West Bank settlements. At this time Prime Minister Netanyahu visited Egypt and met with President Hosni Mubarak, urging him to pressurize Abbas to agree to direct talks. Determined to press ahead with plans for a two-state solution, the Palestinian leadership resolved to ask the international community to recognize an independent Palestinian state with the 1967 borders. Israel protested that this would constitute a violation of the so-called Road Map. In January 2011 Foreign Minister Avigdor Lieberman proposed an interim peace agreement in which a Palestinian state would be created initially on 50 percent of the West Bank with its borders to be determined at a later date. This suggestion was rejected by the Palestinians.

The United Nations and the Palestinians

On 10 February 2011, Israel offered to ease economic and security restrictions against the Palestinians; this would include allowing additional Arab construction in East Jerusalem, permitting the Palestinian Authority security control in seven West Bank cities, and discussing a proposed Palestinian Authority gas field alongside an Israeli installation off the coast of Gaza. Such steps would be conditional on the resumption of peace talks. This plan was agreed to by the Middle East Quartet chief Tony Blair, but rejected by the Palestinians. In response to this scheme, Chief Negotiator Saeb Erekat stated that Israel should stop settlement construction in the West Bank and East Jerusalem and recognize a Palestinian state on the territories occupied in 1967. The next day Israel approved the construction of thirteen additional Jewish homes in an East Jerusalem neighbourhood.

Soon afterwards, the Palestinian Authority announced its plan to request that the United Nations recognize Hebron and Bethlehem as World Heritage Sites. The aim was to curtail growth of Jewish settlements in these cities. On 12 February 2011, Saeb Erekat announced his resignation over the Palestine Papers scandal, which allegedly showed that he had agreed to wide-ranging concessions to Israel on the issues of Jerusalem, refugees, borders and Israeli security. According to Erekat, such documents were false.

On 18 February 2011 the United States vetoed a United Nations Security Resolution condemning Israeli settlement activity. The purpose of this veto was to demonstrate that the Obama administration saw direct negotiation as the only way forward. Israel expressed appreciation for the United States action, whereas the Palestinian Authority condemned what they regarded as American bias. The next month Prime Minister Netanyahu considered a temporary peace deal that envisaged a Palestinian state created with provisional borders, and future borders to be negotiated at a later date. On 3 March the Palestinians rejected this plan, stating that that its position was unaltered.

Due to this impasse in negotiations, the Palestinian Authority declared that unless a deal was reached by September 2011, it would unilaterally declare independence, seek recognition by the United Nations, and apply for membership. According to Mahmoud Abbas, this new state would be ready to negotiate all the core issues and find a just solution for Palestinian refugees in accordance with United Nations General Assembly Resolution 194. Subsequently, the Palestinian Authority refused to restart talks with the Israel or reconsider its intention to declare statehood until the Israeli government froze all settlement construction and agreed to a solution based on the 1967 borders. Further, PLO official Yasser Abed Rabbo claimed that a Palestinian state would not tolerate an Israeli military or civilian presence on its land and would seek UN intervention.

In April 2011, Fatah and Hamas signed a unity agreement, and announced plans to form a government. Israel responded by temporarily freezing the transfer of customs funds Israel collected for the Palestinian Authority; later it released them following guarantees that the money would not be transferred to Hamas. Later Abbas agreed to a French offer to host peace talks by July 2011. Several days later the chairwoman of the US House Foreign Affairs Committee announced plans to introduce legislation that would withhold US contributions to any UN entity that recognizes a Palestinian state or upgrades PLO observer status at the United Nations.

In July 2011, the Quartet on the Middle East convened, but did not produce a statement.

These events were followed by Mahmoud Abbas' submission of an application for the admission of Palestine to the United Nations on the basis of the 4 June 1967 borders with Al-Quds Sharif as its capital. In his speech to the General Assembly on 23 September 2011, he appealed for his people to be given the right to be called citizens of their own state. In the streets of Ramallah, the seat of the Palestinian Authority, the national flag and banners were hung proclaiming the birth of the 194th member of the United Nations. Loudspeakers blared the Palestinian national anthem and there was dancing and celebration in the city's Yasser Arafat Square, where a large crowd had gathered to listen to the president's speech. Palestine, he declared, is intricately linked with the United Nations via the Resolutions adopted by its various organs and agencies and via the role of the United Nations Relief and Works Agency for Palestinian Refugees. Hence, the Palestinians seek a greater and more effective role for the United Nations in working to achieve a just and comprehensive peace that ensures the inalienable, legitimate national rights of the Palestinian people as defined by the resolutions of international legitimacy of the United Nations.

Referring to the most recent negotiations with Israel, Abbas stated that the Palestinians did not cease in their efforts for initiatives and contacts. Over the past year, he said, the Palestinian negotiators did not leave a door to be knocked or a channel to be tested, or a path to be taken. Nor did they ignore any formal or informal party of influence and stature to be addressed. They positively considered the various ideas and proposals and initiatives presented from many countries and parties. Yet, the Israeli government dashed the hopes raised by the launch of negotiations. The core issue was that the Israeli government refuses to commit to terms of reference for the negotiations that are based on international law and United Nations resolutions. Further, it frantically continues to intensify building settlements on the territory of the State of Palestine. Such actions embody the core of the policy of colonial military occupation of the land, and the brutality of aggression and racial discrimination against the Palestinian people. Such a policy is a breach of international law and United Nations resolutions.

Israel's settlement campaign, he continued, is executed through the systematic confiscation of Palestinian lands and the construction of thousands of new settlement units in various areas of the West Bank, particularly in East Jerusalem, as well as the accelerated construction of the annexation Wall that is eating up large tracts of land and dividing it into separate islands and cantons – such a development destroys family life and communities as well as the livelihoods of tens of thousands of families. Israel also continues to refuse permits for the Palestinian people to build in occupied East Jerusalem at the same time as it intensifies its campaign of demolition and confiscation of homes which have displaced Palestinian owners and residents under a prolonged policy of ethnic cleansing. Further, Israel continues to undertake excavations that threaten holy places, and its military checkpoints prevent Palestinian citizens from getting access to their mosques and churches; it also continues to besiege the Holy City with a ring of settlements imposed to separate Jerusalem from the rest of the Palestinian cities.

Israel, he insisted, seeks to redraw the borders of the land according to what it wants and to impose a fait accompli on the ground that undermines the realistic potential for the existence of the State of Palestine. At the same time, Israel continues to impose its blockade on the Gaza Strip and to target Palestinian civilians by assassinations, air strikes and artillery shelling. Israel also continues its incursions in areas of the Palestine National Authority through raids, arrests and killings at the checkpoints. Such policies and actions destroy the chances of achieving a two-state solution, and also threaten to undermine the structure of the Palestinian National Authority.

In the light of this state of affairs, the President on behalf of the Palestinian Liberation Organization – the sole representative of the Palestinian people – stated the following:

(1) The goal of the Palestinian people is the realization of their inalienable national rights in their independent State of Palestine, with East Jerusalem as its capital, on all of the land of the West Bank, including East Jerusalem and the Gaza Strip.

(2) The PLO and the Palestinian people adhere to the renouncement of violence and rejection and condemning of terrorism

in all its forms, especially state terrorism, and adhere to all agreements signed between the Palestine Liberation Organization and Israel.

(3) The Palestinian people adhere to the option of negotiating a lasting solution to the conflict in accordance with resolutions of national legitimacy and the Palestine Liberation Organization is ready to return immediately to the negotiation table on the basis of the adopted terms of reference based on international legitimacy and a complete cessation of settlement activities.

(4) The Palestinian people will continue peaceful resistance to Israeli occupation and its settlement policies and its construction of the annexation Wall.

(5) The Palestinian people rely on the political and diplomatic option and confirm that they do not seek to take unilateral steps.

In conclusion, he stated:

> The time has come for our men, women and children to live normal lives, for them to be able to sleep without waiting for the worst that the next day will bring; for mothers to be assured that their children will return home without fear of suffering, killing, arrest or humiliation; for students to be able to go to their schools and universities without checkpoints obstructing them. The time has come for sick people to be able to reach hospitals normally, and for our farmers to be able to take care of their good land without fear of the occupation seizing the land and its water, which the wall prevents access to, or fear of the settlers, for whom settlements are being built on our land and who are uprooting and burning the olive trees that have existed for hundreds of years. The time has come for the thousands of prisoners to be released from the prisons to return to their families and their children to become part of building their homeland, for the freedom of which they have settled.

> (Haaretz.com, December 29, 2011)

Summary

From the beginnings of the Zionist movement, Arab opponents of Israel have advocated a one-state solution to the Middle-East problem. In their view, Jewish settlers in Palestine were colonialist invaders. For this reason there was no support for early partition plans. Yet more recently there has been growing Palestinian acceptance of a two-state solution. No longer is the PLO determined to eliminate the Jewish state and create in its stead an Arab polity comprising the territory of Israel and the currently occupied West Bank and Gaza Strip. This is the background to the series of negotiations that have taken place in recent years between Jewish and Palestinian representatives. Yet despite the substantial progress that has been made, the gulf between Palestinian aspirations and Israeli demands has prevented a comprehensive agreement from being reached. This deadlock has not only created serious instability in the Middle East but is also a threat to world peace.

Conclusion

In his speech to the United Nations delivered following President Mahmoud Abbas' address on 23 September 2011, Prime Minister Benjamin Netanyahu extended the hand of peace to the Palestinian people. Yet, he stressed that peace must be anchored in security. The truth, he stated, is that a solution to the Middle East crisis cannot be achieved through UN Resolutions, but only through direct negotiations between the parties. Israel, he insisted, wants peace with a Palestinian state, but the Palestinians want a state without peace. As the prime minister of Israel, he was unprepared to risk the future of the Jewish state on wishful thinking.

Outlining the history of negotiations with the Palestinians, Netanyahu cited the offers made in the past, including the withdrawal from Lebanon in 2000 and from Gaza in 2005. Yet, such steps only brought the Islamic storm closer and made it stronger. Hezbollah and Hamas fired thousands of rockets against Israeli cities from the very territories Israel vacated. Given that missiles have rained down on Israel, Israelis ask: 'What's to prevent this from happening again in the West Bank.' The difficulty is that critics press Israel to make far-reaching concessions without first assuring Israel's security.

Serious peace negotiations, Netanyahu insisted, can be properly addressed, but they will not be confronted without negotiations. The

Palestinian leadership insists that Palestine must be a sovereign country: it can never tolerate a long-term military presence in critically strategic areas in the West Bank. But any potential cracks in Israel's security have to be sealed in a peace agreement before a Palestinian state is declared. This must happen first, not afterwards. The Palestinians must first make peace with Israel and then get their state.

A year ago, Netanyahu laid out a vision for peace in which a demilitarized Palestinian state recognizes the Jewish state. But the Palestinians refuse to accept this. Israel has been determined to protect the rights of all its minorities, including more than a million Arab citizens. But the Palestinians refuse to allow any Jews to live on Palestinian soil. Palestine is to be Jew-free. This is nothing less than ethnic cleansing. Laws in Ramallah make the selling of land to Jews punishable by death – this is racism. Israel, however, has no desire to change the democratic nature of the state.

Referring to President Abbas' claim that the core of the Israeli–Palestinian problem is the settlements, Netanyahu stressed that the conflict between Israel and the Palestinians has been raging for nearly half a century. In his view, the core of the conflict is not the settlements; the settlements are a result of the conflict. The conflict has arisen because of the refusal of the Palestinians to recognize a Jewish state on any border. In conclusion, he called on President Abbas to return to negotiations.

> Stop walking around this issue of the Jewish state, and make peace with us. In such a genuine peace, Israel is prepared to make painful compromises. We believe that the Palestinians should be neither the citizens of Israel nor its subjects. They should live in a free state of their own. But they should be ready, like us, for compromises. And we will know that they're ready for compromise and for peace when they start taking Israel's security requirements seriously and when they stop denying our historical connection to our ancient homeland . . . As the prime minister of Israel, I speak for a hundred generations of Jews who were dispersed throughout the lands, who suffered every evil under the sun, but who never gave up hope of restoring their national life in the one and only Jewish state.
>
> (Haaeretz.com, December 31, 2011)

For Jews, the security of Israel is paramount. After nearly 2000 years of exile we have returned to the land of our ancestors. Such a hope sustained the Jewish people through centuries of suffering and persecution. As God's chosen people we have been destined to wander from country to country, always aliens in a majority culture. In a post-Holocaust world we remain committed to insure that the Jewish state will continue and flourish. The true Israel can only prevail if it continues to be vigilant in a hostile world. The patriarch Jacob himself knew that survival was paramount all those years ago when he wrestled with God by the ford of Jabbok. As he limped away from the encounter, he declared: 'I have seen God face to face and still my life is preserved.'

Nonetheless, in our determination to protect our ancestral home, we must not abandon the spiritual tradition that calls us to liberate those who are currently in bondage. The Jewish prophetic tradition highlights the concern for human dignity. The Exodus that we celebrate at Passover reminds us of the eternal obligation to help the oppressed and enslaved. Jewish ethics is a morality of praxis, of concrete action in the present. We must not stand aloof from human degradation. As an empowered people, it is our duty to empower those who remain in exile, as we were for nearly twenty centuries. This is the moral background to a consideration of the problem of Middle East politics.

Today we stand on the threshold of a new era. Despite the repeated failure of a two-state solution to the conflict between Israel and the Palestinians, there is now the opportunity to achieve a lasting and just peace in the region. It is, as Prime Minister Netanyahu emphasized, time for serious and painful compromise from both sides. However, Israel has not agreed to the Palestinian demand to stop building settlements. A resolution has been submitted to the United Nations for recognition of Palestinian statehood. In a formal letter to Ban Ki-Moon, Secretary General of the United Nations, President Abbas wrote:

> I have the profound honour, on behalf of the Palestinian people to submit this application of the State of Palestine for admission to membership in the United Nations. This application for membership is being based on the Palestinian people's

natural, legal and historical rights based on United Nations General Assembly resolution 181 (II) of 29 November 1947 as well as the Declaration of Independence of the State of Palestine of 15 November 1988 and the acknowledgement by the General Assembly of this Declaration in resolution 43/177 of 15 December 1988. In this connection, the State of Palestine is committed to the achievement of a just, lasting and comprehensive resolution of the Israeli–Palestinian conflict based on the vision of two-states living side by side in peace and security, as endorsed by the United Nations Security Council and General Assembly and the international community as a whole and based on international law and all relevant United Nations resolutions.

(www.scribd.com/com/doc/66184173/S.G-Letter-on-Palestine-Membership)

President Netanyahu asserts that negotiation must precede statehood. Yet the recognition of the Palestinian statehood (without a designation of borders) and of membership of Palestine in the community of nations should be a first step on the road to peace. What should follow is intense serious negotiations of all the issues that will call for serious and painful compromise on the part of both Israel and the Palestinians. Let us embrace this first step toward solving what has been unsolvable in the past. In the year 2012 let us turn swords into ploughshares, before it is too late.

Dawoud El-Alami with Dan Cohn-Sherbok

Bibliography

Bauer, Y., *From Diplomacy to Resistance: A History of Jewish Palestine 1939–1945*, New York, Atheneum, 1973.

Caplan, Neil, *Palestine Jewry and the Arab Question 1917–1925*, London, Routledge, 1978.

Chomsky, Noam, *The Fateful Triangle: The United States, Israel, and the Palestinians*, Boston, South End Press, 1983.

Chomsky, Noam, *Gaza in Crisis: Reflections on Israel's War Against the Palestinians*, New York, Simon and Schuster, 2011.

Cohn-Sherbok, Dan and El-Alami, Dawoud, *The Palestine–Israeli Conflict*, Oxford, Oneworld, 2006.

Dershowitz, Alan, *The Case for Israel*, Hoboken, NJ, John Wiley and Sons, 2004.

Ellis, Marc, *Towards a Jewish Theology of Liberation*, Baylor, Baylor University Press, 2004.

Ellis, Marc, *Israel and Palestine: Out of the Ashes. The Search for Jewish Identity in the Twenty-First Century*, London, Pluto Press, 2002.

Fackenheim, E., *The Jewish Thought of Emil Fackenheim*, edited by Michael Morgan, Detroit, Wayne State University Press, 1987.

Finkelstein, Louis, *Haggadah of Passover*, New York, Hebrew Publishing Co., 1942.

Finkelstein, Norman, *Image and Reality of the Israel-Palestine Conflict*, New York, Penguin, 2001.

Frankel, W., *Israel Observed: An Anatomy of the State*, London, Thames and Hudson, 1980.

Gaon, Saadya, *The Book of Doctrines and Beliefs*, New Haven, Yale University Press, 1948.

Gilbert, Martin, *Israel: A History*, London, Black Swan, 1999.

Hiro, D., *Sharing the Promised Land: An Interwoven Tale of Israelis and Palestinians*, London, Hodder and Stoughton, 1996.

Goldberg, David, *To The Promised Land: A History of Zionist Thought from Its Origin to the Modern State of Israel*, London, Penguin, 1996.

Goodman, Phillip (ed.), *The Passover Anthology*, Philadelphia, Jewish Publication Society, 1961.

Halevi, Judah, *The Kuzari*, New York, Schocken, 1964.

Ha-Am, Ahad, *Essays, Letters, Essays, Memoirs*, Oxford, Oxford University Press, 1946.

Heschel, A., *The Prophets*, 2 vols, New York, Harper & Row 1969–1971.

Joseph, M., *Judaism as Creed and Life*, London, Macmillan, 1903.

Kohler, Kaufmann, *Jewish Theology*, New York, KTAV, 1968.

Laqueur, Walter, *A History of Zionism*, London, Weidenfeld and Nicholson, 1972.

Laqueur, Walter, Rubin, B. (eds), *The Israel–Arab Reader*, London, Penguin, 1995.

Lazarus, M., *The Ethics of Judaism*, Philadelphia, Jewish Publication Society, 1900.

Lucas, N., *The Modern History of Israel*, London, Praeger, 1975.

Mandel, N.J., *The Arabs and Zionism before World War I*, Berkeley, University of California Press, 1976.

Masalha, N., *Imperial Israel and the Palestinians: The Politics of Expansion*, London, Pluto Press, 2000.

Morris, Benny, *One State, Two States*, London, Yale University Press, 2009.

Naor, A., 'Greate Israel', in Benny Morris, *One State, Two States*, London, Yale University Press, 2009.

O'Brien, Conor Cruise, *The Siege: The Saga of Israel and Zionism*, London, Paladin, 1988.

Pappe, I., *The Israel/Palestine Question*, London, Routledge, 1999.

Porath, Yehoshua, *The Emergence of the Palestinian–Arab National Movement 1918–1929*, London, Frank Cass, 1974.

Rodinson, M., *Israel and the Arabs*, London, Penguin, 1982.

Rosenzweig, Franz, *The Star of Redemption*, Notre Dame, IN, University of Notre Dame, 1985.

Sachar, Howard M., *A History of Israel from the Rise of Zionism to Our Time*, New York, Alfred A. Knopf, 2007.

Said, E. *The End of the Peace Process: Oslo and After*, New York, Vintage, 2001.

Schechter, Solomon, *Aspects of Rabbinic Theology: Major Concepts of the Talmud*, New York, Schocken, 1961.

Shahak, I., and Mezvinsky, N., *Jewish Fundamentalism in Israel*, London, Pluto Press, 2004.

Shindler, Colin, *Ploughshares into Swords? Israelis and Jews in the Shadow of the Intifada*, London, I.B. Taurus, 1991.

Shlaim, Avi, *Israel and Palestine*, London, Verso, 2010.

Sizer, Stephen, *Christian Zionism: Road Map to Armageddon*, London, InterVarsity Press, 2005.

Spero, S., *Morality, Halakha and the Jewish Tradition*, New York, KTAV, 1983.

Stein, Leslie, *The Making of Modern Israel 1948–1967*, Cambridge, Polity Press, 2009.

Vital, David, *Origins of Zionism*, Oxford, Clarendon Press, 1980.

Vital, David, *Zionism: The Formative Years*, Oxford, Clarendon Press, 1982.

Vital, David, *Zionism, The Crucial Phase*, Oxford, Clarendon Press, 1987.

Wasserstein, B., *The British in Palestine*, London, Royal Historical Society, 1979.

Index